Yale University Faculty Comments from 1939:

...you have done an excellent job in presenting the history of this community and its relation to the larger community, the city of Stamford. Your work impresses me as being quite authoritative....there are altogether too few studies of ethnic groups available and I believe none that treats of a Jewish community...your book will be especially opportune at this time when nationalism and racialism are rampant. Your impartial and objective study should do much to promote mutual knowledge and respect...

Maurice R. Davie

...your excellent essay on the Jews of Stamford represents a carefully planned and executed work. My own experience in the study and teaching of sociological material concerning American minority groups has shown me that investigations...of specific communities are scarce and much needed. Your sponsors should be gratified by the results of your research in the community.

Raymond Kennedy

...a careful and scholarly piece of work. Studies of this type should make for an improved understanding of some of our ethnic groups and their problems. So far as I know, yours is the first adequate study of a Jewish community in the United States, and it gives a vivid picture of the organization of the group and of its adjustment to American society.

George P. Murdock

AN AMERICAN JEWISH COMMUNITY

50 YEARS
1889-1939

THE SOCIOLOGY OF THE JEWISH COMMUNITY IN
IN STAMFORD, CONNECTICUT

BY

SAMUEL KOENIG, PH.D

FOR

WORK PROJECTS ADMINISTRATION
FEDERAL WRITERS PROJECT FOR
THE STATE OF CONNECTICUT
1940

Stamford Jewish Historical Society
Stamford, Connecticut
1991

Copyright © 1991 by
Stamford Jewish Historical Society

Designed and Produced by Romax Communications, Stamford CT
Cover Design by Joel Tanner

Library of Congress Cataloging-in-Publication Data

Koenig, Samuel 1899-1972
An American Jewish Community
    50 Years 1889-1939
The Sociology of the Jewish Community in
Stamford, Connecticut

    p.   cm.
    Includes index and bibliographic reference
ISBN 0-9629560-0-7

1. Sociology - Economics
2. Jews — Community - Religious institutions
3. History — Stamford, Connecticut to 1939 with additional
    material to 1991
4. Ethnic group

    F104. S8K64 1991   91-3998
    974.6'9--dc20   CIP

Manufactured in the United States of America
Printed on acid free paper

To the memory of those anonymous
workers who collected the data
for the ethnic studies of the
Federal Writers Project

TABLE OF CONTENTS

LIST OF TABLES

LIST OF TABLES
(Contined)

LIST OF TABLES
(Contined)

LIST OF CHARTS

LIST OF ILLUSTRATIONS

PREFACE

The story of how Samuel Koenig's report, completed in 1940, came to be published fifty-one years later is an interesting example of serendipity. In 1983, after considerable effort, Professor Christopher Collier, with Bonnie B. Collier, filled issue No. 6 of the Connecticut Scholar with an exhaustive The *Literature of Connecticut History*. Included in this volume was a reference to a study of the Jews of Stamford done in the 1930s under the Federal Writer's Project — "A superb study of Stamford Jews made by Samuel Koenig...under WPA auspices." Ron Marcus, Librarian of the Stamford Historical Society, noticed this item and contacted Lester Sharlach of the Stamford Jewish Historical Society. At the end of 1986 they went to the Connecticut State Library in Hartford to locate the study. They were successful and were able to have a copy made of the two hundred page typescript.

The Stamford Jewish Historical Society circulated the copy among a few members, who felt that this work would be of great interest to the Stamford Jewish Community and should be distributed, locally. As a result, a decision was made to print the typescript.

The first task was to obtain a legible copy of the typescript. The available technology of computer scanning the copy of a copy failed to produce a useful data file. The only alternative was to retype the typescript. This was done by several data entry operators, who produced a number of typographical errors. Correcting these files required considerable efforts by Julian Reitman, Paula Eppinger, and Evelyn Fowler. In the process, Julian Reitman also produced the index.

One result of having a clean copy was the emergence of the concept that Koenig's document would be of interest far beyond the local area. There is a dearth of sociological and economic data detailing the existence of an entire Jewish community during the Great Depression. When the Stamford Jewish Historical Society attempted to find a university press, none of those contacted were interested.

While all this was proceeding, Irwin Miller was making some investigations into the earliest Jews in Stamford and uncovered additional data that expanded upon Koenig's information. It was decided to add this new material as an additional set of notes using { } symbols. In keeping with the concept of a changing Jewish community, an Epilogue was compiled by Marvin Paymer from responses distributed to current Jewish organizations by the Stamford Jewish Historical Society.

Koenig's typescript suggested some illustrations. However, none were found in the State Library files. Arnold Yelin, Lester Sharlach, Irwin Miller, and Julian Reitman selected illustrations which retained the flavor originally suggested. Pictures were obtained from the Stamford Historical Society, Ferguson Library, and Stamford Jewish Historical Society. Bill Gottlin wrote the introduction.

George Goldberg, the current president of the Stamford Jewish Historical Society, has coordinated the project throughout the long gestation period. He was encouraged in this effort by numerous other individuals in many different ways to support this effort by a dedicated group of volunteers.

Koenig Report Committee

Julian Reitman, Chairman
Paula Eppinger
Evelyn Fowler
William Gottlin
George Goldberg
Irwin Miller
Marvin Paymer
Lester Sharlach
Arnold Yelin

INTRODUCTION

In 1938, Samuel Koenig, director of the Connecticut Ethnic Survey, conducted a study of the Jewish community in Stamford. Titled *An American Jewish Community: The Story of the Jews in Stamford, Connecticut,* Koenig's goal was to give a comprehensive historical, economic and social picture of a Jewish community, with special emphasis on the organizations and institutions that Stamford's Jews had created to help them assimilate into American society while preserving their cultural heritage.

Koenig was sponsored by the Stamford Jewish Center, and he enjoyed widespread cooperation from the Jewish community in compiling the demographic data that was at the heart of his project. Yet, at a meeting of the Board of Directors of the Stamford Jewish Center in 1940, Koenig's manuscript was rejected as too controversial, and the Center withdrew its sponsorship. Two abridged versions of the study were subsequently published, but the complete manuscript remained unpublished, forgotten for almost fifty years in the archives of the Connecticut State Library.[1]

Samuel Koenig was himself a model for the community he was writing about. Born in Monasterzyska, Austria-Hungary in 1899, he emigrated to the United States in 1921. Koenig attended the University of Minnesota and graduated from Marquette University in 1929. In 1935 Koenig earned a Ph.D. degree from Yale University, and in 1936 obtained a prominent position with the Federal Writers Project (FWP), which had just been formed as part of the Work Projects Administration (WPA), a New Deal agency charged with putting America's millions of unemployed to work.

The FWP's first and most well-known effort was the writing of a series of state guidebooks. Henry Alsberg, the FWP's director, believed that the guidebooks should be supplemented with social and ethnic studies. In response, the Connecticut Ethnic Survey was organized. Koenig was appointed as director of the Survey. The Survey's goal was to understand the immigrants on their own terms, and in doing so shed light on contemporary America. This was especially relevant to Connecticut, where almost two-thirds of the population were foreigners or first generation Americans.

Koenig's work moved along two tracks. Statistical data were gathered on immigrant groups, and fieldworkers collected oral histories of the immigrants' lives. Although Alsberg had hoped that the ethnic surveys would favor the "human angle" as opposed to more academic statistical studies,[2] Koenig's first publication in 1938 relied heavily on statistical sources. *Immigrant Settlements In Connecticut: Their Growth And Characteristics* was a survey of seventeen immigrant groups in Connecticut, offered as "a bird's eye view of our immigrant communities."[3] A comprehensive study of immigrant groups, including oral histories, was planned.[4]

Meanwhile, Koenig's attention had been drawn to a specific ethnic group, the Jews of Stamford. His motivation for studying this group is not known, although he had a lifelong involvement in Jewish affairs, which included writing a number of scholarly papers on Jewish topics, serving on commissions on Jewish education, and teaching in Israel. He was interested in the process of the immigrants' assimilation (certainly this must have pertained to him personally as well). Of course, Koenig's work with the Ethnic Survey also justified the Stamford study.

Koenig secured the support of the Stamford Jewish Center as co-sponsor with the State of Connecticut, and on May 17, 1938, the Center's President, Noah Adler, made formal application to the Federal Writers Project to publish and distribute the work when it was completed.[5]

The work was predominantly done by Koenig, and he requested that his name appear as author instead of the customary credit to the "Workers of the Connecticut Writers' Project." In a 1940 memo to Louise Crampton, state supervisor of the Connecticut Writers Project, justifying his request for authorship, Koenig wrote, in the third person, that he had "conceived of the idea of making a sociological study of the Jewish community of Stamford, Connecticut. After assuring himself of the approval and cooperation of the local community, he was given the special assignment of planning, doing the research, and of writing the book, which he did. No other person on the Project did any writing on it, and the work is a strictly one-man job."[6] Koenig's name appeared alone on the completed manuscript.

A year later, Koenig wrote that "the chief sources have been interviews with well-informed residents, first hand observation, and available records and publications. The demographic part is mainly the result of an actual census of the Jews in the community, taken in the latter part of 1938. Using printed schedules, the essential information has been obtained directly from all but 36 of the 960 families comprising the community."[7]

Some of Koenig's sources may have been the nine Federal Writers Project fieldworkers in the Stamford area in late 1938.[8] Perhaps the most helpful was Sholom Sontup, a Strawberry Hill Avenue resident with a reputation as a Jewish scholar. Sontup wrote a 24 page survey of eastern European Jews in the 1800's[9] that Koenig adapted for *An American Jewish Community.* In a later condensation of this work, Koenig acknowledged Sontup, "a resident of the town at the time, for his invaluable assistance in compiling the data for the present study."[10]

Koenig sent drafts of his study to a number of professors, including M.R. Davie, head of Yale's Department of Sociology, and Dr. Solomon Goldman, a Chicago rabbi and President of the Zionist Organization of America, who suggested changes and strongly approved of the work.[11] Several professors wrote letters of recommendation to Koenig. Davie wrote, "there are altogether too few studies of ethnic groups available and I believe none that treats of a Jewish community...I think your book will be especially opportune at this time when nationalism and racialism are rampant."[12] Sociology Professor Raymond Kennedy of Yale University wrote, "Your sponsors should be gratified by the results of your research in the community."[13]

The completed work was awaiting publication in 1940. Five hundred copies were slated to be printed,[14] with possible distribution to Jewish institutions, libraries and Jewish social workers, among others.[15]

Preparations came to a screeching halt at the April 16, 1940 Board Meeting of the Stamford Jewish Center. After reviewing Koenig's work, the Board decided to cancel their sponsorship, and Executive Director William Pinsker told Koenig of their decision. Koenig attempted to make his work more acceptable, and in June wrote to his supervisor, Louise Crampton, that "the study has been gone over painstakingly with the members of the advisory board of the Stamford Jewish community and all inaccuracies or passages deemed misleading or harsh eliminated."[16] This was to no avail.

Ten months later, in a February 14, 1941 letter to Crampton, Pinsker explained the Board's decision. Pinsker wrote, "many of the viewpoints and general tenor of the work are not only of a controversial nature, but contrary to the attitudes of so many of our members, that we could not give it our backing without antagonising (sic) substantial numbers by a sponsorship to which they object."[17]

Koenig, meanwhile, had left the FWP in 1941 for a faculty job with the Department of Sociology and Anthropology at Brooklyn College. *An American Jewish Community,* revised and retitled "The Socio-Economic Structure of an American Jewish Community," was published in an anthology of Jewish studies called *Jews in a Gentile World* in 1942. In 1948, a 29 page segment of the study was published as "The Jews of Easterntown: The Genesis of Jewish Community Life In An American Town," in a periodical called the *Jewish Review.*[18] Koenig went on to a long and distinguished career as a professor at Brooklyn College and author of numerous sociological books and articles.[19]

What made *An American Jewish Community* so controversial? The Jewish community, like many other predominantly immigrant groups, was sensitive about its image. This was exacerbated by the rise of anti-Semitism in Europe. Perhaps some in the Jewish community feared that Koenig's study, which portrayed the Jews as a relatively prosperous part of the Stamford community, would leave them vulnerable to an anti-Semitic backlash. The members of the Jewish Center may not have welcomed an airing of "dirty laundry," such as the discussion of Jewish criminality, or the taint of Jewish involvement in socialist causes. Koenig's extensive review of the political and religious divisions in the Jewish community, and his assessment of various groups (for example, the religious laxity of Temple Beth-El, or the Zionists' preeminence) might have led to fractious arguments. Koenig's discussion of relations with the Christian community, which included examples of anti-Jewish discrimination in several occupational categories and social clubs, might have also led to concerns of "stirring up trouble."

An American Jewish Community is divided into two parts. Part One (chapters I-VI) offers an historical overview of Stamford, eastern European Jewry, and a history of the Jewish community in Stamford. Part Two (chapters VII-XI) presents a contemporary analysis of the Jews of Stamford as of 1938. Although Part One provides much of interest, Part Two delivers what is unique to this work: an original, comprehensive survey of the Jewish community. Koenig and his helpers found out about the occupations, religious beliefs, marriages, politics and social life of the Jewish community. Little escaped his sociological microscope. Koenig's conclusions may be debated (as they certainly were at the time he presented this work to the Jewish Center); certain topics may seem dryly descriptive rather than interpretive; and the great mass of data he collected sometimes overwhelmed attempts at organization. It cannot be denied, however, that Koenig's work is rich in detail.

Chapter I gives a brief overview of Stamford, and Koenig pointed out that 69% of "Yankee" Stamford's population were of foreign birth or parentage. Chapter II shifts to a description of the culture and plight of eastern European Jews, which has intrinsic interest but is only indirectly connected to the rest of the book.[20] Chapter III returns to Stamford, and there is interesting material on the early Jewish settlers in Stamford, who, it is shown, did not create a Jewish communal life (Irwin Miller's footnotes reveal that there were Jews in Stamford even earlier than Koenig and his researchers imagined). Chapter IV gives a brief sketch of everyday life in Stamford in the 1880's.

Koenig began to develop the main theme of *An American Jewish Community* in Chapter V, which was the building of the Jewish community by the poor, eastern European Jewish peddlers and shopkeepers who gathered in Stamford from the 1880's. Koenig established the beginning of the community with the organizing of the Agudath Sholom congregation in 1889, and the burial society and Society for Welcoming Transients in 1891. Chapter VI completes the historical background, and traces the growth of the Jewish community. As it grew, the community began to fissure along political (Zionist and socialist) and religious (orthodox and conservative) lines, themes that Koenig elaborated on in subsequent chapters. Koenig established that the Zionists were the most dynamic group in the Jewish community. In 1916 they bought a building for their school that was to become the Hebrew Institute. The growing religious divisions, which reflected in part the split between those who clung to the traditional ways and those who were "Americanized," led to the building of Temple Beth-El in 1927. Common ground for all groups was the new Jewish Community Center, completed in 1930.

The extraordinary statistical analysis in Chapter VII is based on a door-to-door survey of every Jewish family in town, to which over 96% responded. A wealth of information follows from this exuberant response. Fifty-five percent of the Jewish families were headed by a foreign-born parent, but two-thirds of Stamford's Jews were American-born (the parents were foreign, the children native). Forty-five percent were between 21 to 44 years old. Only 21 families reported that none of their members were employed, in the midst of the Great Depression. About 30% of the Jews owned their homes. Some of the most vivid statistics show the economic side of the Jewish community. Most Jews were employed in trade and commerce or were professionals. Less than 9% worked in factories in a factory town. Jews dominated certain businesses: 13 of 15 men's furnishings shops; 22 of 30 women's and misses' clothing dealers; 10 of 19 shoe stores; 13 of 15 jewelry stores. In the professions, 48 of 110 lawyers were Jewish, and there were a good number of Jewish doctors, dentists and teachers. Koenig also noted that Jewish lawyers were limited to less lucrative legal work, and Jews were under-represented in banks, insurance and real estate.

Chapter VIII is focused on the central institution of the Jewish community, the Jewish Center. Koenig wrote that the idealogical basis for the Center was the need to preserve Jewish cultural heritage, but the reason for its success was that it provided a social outlet for a community still isolated from their Christian neighbors. Few of the Center's events were specifically Jewish in nature, but took place in a "Jewish atmosphere," and therefore became Jewish functions. Koenig believed that the Center's programs acted to encourage assimilation into the American way of life.

Koenig's strong interest in Jewish education and youth activities led him into a lengthy discussion of some of the 27 organizations, including a formal school, that the Center maintained. He clearly showed that Jewish education was one of the primary political battlegrounds between the Zionists and the socialists, the orthodox and conservative, the foreign and native-born.

Chapter IX detailed the ideological divisions in the Jewish community. Koenig established that the Zionists, who supported a Jewish homeland, were the dominant group, as evidenced by their eight organizations with over 600 members. The most active group was Hadassah, with 361 women and girls, and the most important male group was the Brandeis Club, with 87 business and professional men, including 22 members of the board of directors of the Community Center. Conversely, Koenig took pains to establish that "socialism as a movement in the Jewish community has never been strong and at present is all but dead." The careful reader will have some reason to believe that the socialists were not quite buried. Koenig, with typical attention to detail, wrote that the socialist-oriented Workmens' Circle had 65 members, the communist International Workers Order had 45 members, the Young Communist League had 10 Jewish members and there were 32 Jewish communists of unspecified affiliation. In addition, two groups linked with the Zionists, the National Workers' Alliance and the Jewish Pioneer Women, were in fact socialist-Zionists, and they had 158 members.

Koenig also reviewed the mutual aid societies, those once-common immigrant organizations that provided burial and sick benefits and companionship. The largest was the Independent Stamford Lodge with 175 members. Providing an illuminating look at the social structure of Stamford in the 1930's, Koenig discussed Jewish involvement in non-Jewish social clubs. While Jews were prominent in several clubs, there were instances of anti-Jewish discrimination; Koenig wrote of the Roosevelt Lodge, which was founded by Jews who were blackballed by the existing Masonic lodges in Stamford.

Koenig plunged into the religious differences in the Jewish community in Chapter X. His statistics showed that membership in the orthodox and conservative congregations was roughly equal, with more families belonging to neither. Koenig observed that traditional ways were being abandoned or modified, which he understood as adaptions to new circumstances. Koenig found Temple Beth El too lax in religious observance, and following unessential practices, such as organ music and weekly sermons by the rabbi. Likewise, Agudath Sholom was criticised for failing to keep up with new trends in the Jewish community.

Chapter XI may be the most intriguing section of the book. A number of interesting facts and trends are thrown together with scant analysis. We learn that only 10% of Stamford's Jews were not citizens or declarants. Fifty-one percent of all Jewish families were bilingual, speaking Yiddish and English in the home. Despite the documented Zionist control of Jewish cultural life, 141 Stamford Jews subscribed to socialist or radical publications (365 subscribed to Zionist publications). There is information on Jewish-Gentile marriages, criminal and juvenile delinquency cases involving Jewish residents. We are told about the

Hebrew Ladies Educational League, which attended to needy families and dispensed money, food and clothing with "the greatest of secrecy."

Koenig concluded that the Jews were a vital part of the Stamford community, and they were evolving from an immigrant community to an American one. The Jewish community is still evolving, and so this valuable book serves as a benchmark for where we stood 50 years ago, and a reminder of the debt we owe to preceding generations.

William J. Gottlin
Stamford, Connecticut

Footnotes

1 *New York Times,* December 31, 1972.

2 Jerre Mangione, *The Dream and The Deal, The Federal Writers Project 1935-1943* (Boston: Little, Brown and Co., 1972), pp. 277-278.

3 Samuel Koenig, *Immigrant Settlements In Connecticut: Their Growth and Characteristics* (Hartford: Connecticut State Department of Education, 1938), n.p.

4 Laura Anker has written about the importance of oral histories in understanding immigrant lives. She pointed out that the promise of the narratives was largely unfulfilled. An estimated 10,000 WPA oral histories were done, and most of them remained unused or were lost. ("Immigrant Voices From the Federal Writers Project: The Connecticut Ethnic Survey 1937-1940," in *American Society and Culture,* ed. Amy Gilman, David Scott, Joan Scott, James Gilbert, R. Jackson Wilson (Forthcoming).

5 "Application for Permission To Publish," Box 102, WPA Archives, State Library, Hartford, CT.

6 Samuel Koenig to Louise M. Crampton, June 26, 1940, Box 102, WPA Archives, State Library, Hartford, CT.

7 Samuel Koenig, "The Socio-Economic Structure Of An American Jewish Community," Box 102, WPA Archives, State Library, Hartford, CT.

8 They were Patten Beard of Norwalk, Rhoda Cameron of Springdale, Herbert Lee Conner of Darien, and Anna Bivona, Henry Gogay, Helen Huben, Aida C. Parker, Sholom Sontup and Joseph B. Weinstein of Stamford. ("Stamford District," November 16, 1938, Box 102, WPA Archives, State Library, Hartford, CT.)

9 Sholom Sontup, "Notes on East-European Jews of the Nineteenth Century," Federal Writers' Project Ethnic Survey, (unpublished, n.d.)

10 Samuel Koenig, "The Jews Of Easterntown: The Genesis of Jewish Community Life In An American Town," the *Jewish Review,* Vol. V, No. 1-4, (Jan.-Dec. 1948), p.1.

11 Koenig to Crampton, June 26, 1940.

12 Maurice R. Davie to Samuel Koenig, August 10, 1939, Box 102, WPA Archives, State Library, Hartford, CT.

13 Raymond Kennedy to Samuel Koenig, July 13, 1939, Box 102, WPA Archives, State Library, Hartford, CT.

14 "List of Completed Works Awaiting Publication," Box 102, WPA Archives, State Library, Hartford, CT.

15 Box 102, WPA Archives, State Library, Hartford, CT.

16 Koenig to Crampton, June 26, 1940.

17 William Pinsker to Louise Crampton, February 14 1941, Box 102, WPA Archives, State Library, Hartford, CT.

18 Koenig, Samuel, "The Socio-Economic Structure of an American Jewish Community," in Isacque Graeber and Steuart H. Britt, eds., *Jews in a Gentile World* (New York: Macmillan & Co., 1942). Koenig, Samuel, "The Jews of Easterntown: The Genesis of Jewish Community Life In An American Town," in the *Jewish Review,* Vol. V, No. 1-4 (Jan.-Dec., 1948), pp. 1-29.

19 *Times,* December 31, 1972.

20 In "Socio-Economic Structure," Koenig deleted this chapter, along with Chapters IV, V and VI. In "The Jews of Easterntown," Koenig put back most of the historical information, and deleted the contemporary analysis.

CHAPTER I

A GLIMPSE OF THE CITY

Stamford is one of the oldest towns in New England. Settled by a handful of pioneers from Wethersfield in 1641, only twenty-one years after the landing of the Mayflower, Stamford existed up to the middle of the past century as a simple rural community serving as a trading post for the farming country surrounding it. Although a stop-over place for the New York to Boston coaches, it was little affected by the rising metropolis only a short distance away. In the 1840's, however, with the laying of the railroad tracks, its tranquil atmosphere began to be disturbed, and with the completion of the road in 1849 it rapidly lost its rural character.

Situated on the Long Island Sound in an area rich in natural beauty, Stamford is only thirty miles from the heart of New York City. Its many beautiful homes have earned it the names of "City of Quality" and "Garden Spot of Connecticut." Although located in Connecticut, it belongs to that vast suburban area called metropolitan New York, for the more than one hundred daily passenger trains, connecting Stamford with New York within less than an hour, have brought the town into even closer contact with the metropolis than some of the latter's own far-flung sections.

The proximity to New York City coupled with the advantages of its location on the main trunk and railway lines between New York and Boston has had far reaching implications for Stamford. With the growth of New York City and the development of transportation facilities, an increasing number of New York business and professional people turned to Stamford as a place of residence, and many Stamford residents began commuting to their places of business in New York. Stamford has thus become one of those commuting towns so abundant around New York.

Nevertheless, Stamford has preserved its own individuality. Its New England character is still quite apparent in its historic spots, charming colonial houses and the general plan of what constituted formerly the town. The primarily residential nature of the town is evident from its many beautiful homes, fine institutions, parks and beaches. At the same time, its many small and large industries, well hidden behind the railroad embankment, have made it an important manufacturing center.

In the center of the city where the two main thoroughfares, Main and Atlantic Streets, meet, is located the business section which extends in all directions for several blocks. Atlantic Square, the former site of the first meeting-house, whipping posts, stocks, and pillory, is the focal point. Facing the Square, or only a short distance away from it, are situated the most important public buildings, among which the gray-stone Town Hall is the most conspicuous.

The residential sections are grouped around the business area, with the more exclusive ones in the outlying districts. Only a few blocks from the center is Strawberry Hill Avenue with its beautiful residences and delightful flower gardens. Shippan, stretching along the bay and culminating in Shippan Point, is Stamford's most exclusive residential section. Here are located the palatial homes of the wealthy New Yorkers and Stamfordites. High Ridge and Long Ridge are two other districts of handsome residences and extensive estates. Still another attractive residential section is Glenbrook to the northeast, occupied largely by middle class people.

Stamford has, of course, its cheaper neighborhoods as well as its sections of ethnic and racial concentration. At one time these were well defined, as the various names like "Dublin" and "Algiers," still lingering, indicate. But at present strict lines of demarcation have largely disappeared, the only ones remaining being those denoting economic status. Stamford also has its slum area, mostly populated by Negroes. As usual, the housing conditions among those in the lower-income brackets are far from desirable, although a government low-cost housing project has recently been completed providing homes for 146 families. On the other hand, the fact that this is the first project of this nature undertaken in the State undoubtedly reflects the progressive spirit of the city.

In population Stamford ranks sixth among the cities of the State. According to the United States Census of 1930, Stamford

City had 46,346 and Stamford Town, which includes the city, 56,765 inhabitants. This represents an increase of over 41 per cent in the decade of 1920-1930. In comparison with other Connecticut cities, states a survey conducted by the town's Community Chest in 1938, Stamford has "a high median monthly rental, with a low percentage of families paying the rent in the lower brackets." In general, continues the same survey, "the families of Stamford seemed to be rather better off economically than the families of the State."

Approximately one-fifth of the town's population is directly employed by the various large and small factories existing in the town and its immediate vicinity. The articles manufactured in Stamford are of a great variety, the most important being hardware, electric hoists, lacquer articles, motors and generators, ball and roller bearings, boats, oil burning equipment, electric shavers, office equipment, rubber toys, and women's dresses. As elsewhere, production has been considerably cut since the depression, and in some cases employment had been reduced by a third or more. Nevertheless, Yale and Towne, famous for the Yale lock, employs even at present 2,650 workers; Conde-Nast Publications, just outside the Stamford city limits, 1200; Shick Dry Shaver, 700; Norma Hoffman, manufacturer of ball bearings, 600; the Pitney Bowes Company, manufacturer of office equipment, 475; the Atlas Powder Company, 375; and Freydberg Brothers, manufacturer of lacquer articles, 250. Many smaller establishments employ between 50 and 100 workers.

Stamford's population, like that of most of the other towns in Connecticut, is predominately of foreign stock, 32,281, or 69 per cent, being of foreign birth or of foreign or mixed parentage. The largest of the foreign groups are the Italians, Irish, Poles, and Jews. These and a number of smaller immigrant groups give the town that cosmopolitan atmosphere so characteristic of present-day Connecticut. Only 2.5 per cent of Stamford's population is Negro. But this percentage is much higher than the 1.8 per cent for the State as a whole or than that for every other major city in Connecticut, except New Haven and Hartford.

Up to the middle of the past century, Stamford had a homogeneous population consisting almost totally of British stock. The building of the railroad in the 1840's marked the beginning of Irish migration into the town. Up to the early 1880's the Irish constituted the only numerically important non-English immigrant group in the town. The rise of large-scale industry, particularly the expansion of the Yale and Towne factory, and the laying of the parallel railroad lines and subsequent electrification of the road, brought in immigrants from Western and Eastern Europe. It was not, however, till the late 1880's that those from Eastern Europe started coming in, and not until the begining of the present century that any considerable number settled in the town. It was during this period that the Jewish community began taking root.

CHAPTER II

IN THE OLD WORLD

The saying that "Man doth not live by bread alone" is a truth which only emphasizes the fact that it is aliment, food, upon which life depends. In search of it man will go through every hardship. To increase, so to speak, his food rations, he is willing to leave home, cherished places, and cross deserts and oceans — providing he is aware that somewhere there exist better opportunities. It is only when he has enough to eat that he begins to think and then to believe that other things, like freedom, are also essential. Few people, therefore, leave places to which they have been attached with a thousand ties, merely to gain liberty, although this may serve as a motive for some bold spirits. Mass movements, even of minor proportions, occur largely in response to a need for better economic conditions.

If we examine closely the motives for the coming of the various groups to these shores, not excluding the passengers on the Mayflower, we can easily discover that they were essentially economic in nature. To be sure, the intensity of the economic distress forcing people to forsake their homes varies considerably from group to group but this only brings out the fact that even comparatively slight improvement of the economic status will serve as a motive for emigration. Thus, while the Irish were driven here by actual famine, the Scandinavians came here primarily because of prospects for better earnings and promptly stopped coming when conditions in their homelands improved. The Germans were economically better off than, say, the Ukrainians, but it can safely be said that members of both of these groups sought this country for essentially the same reasons.

This, of course, does not imply the absence of other factors of importance. The most significant of these is the scourge of modern man — persecution for economic, racial, religious or political reasons. But here again, unless oppression definitely interferes with an individual's pursuit of a livelihood, few people will take to emigration. Finally, emigration always presupposes the existence of better opportunities somewhere else, the awareness of the prospective emigrant of such a land, and his ability to get there. In the light of the aforesaid let us consider briefly the conditions that prompted the present-day Jewish inhabitant of Stamford or his parents to come to America and eventually to Stamford.

The immigrant Jews of Stamford are derived mainly from provinces of the former Russian and Austro-Hungarian empires and Rumania. There are practically no German or other Western European Jews among them, nor any descendants of early Spanish-Portuguese Jews. The following description of conditions under which the Jews were living prior to their coming to this country will therefore be confined to those prevailing in the three above-mentioned countries. Again, since the exodus of Jews from those countries began in the eighties of the past century, our sketch will be limited to a portrayal of conditions prevalent at that time.

The great bulk of the population of Eastern Europe under the domination of the Russian and Austro-Hungarian empires did not emerge from actual serfdom until the latter part of the nineteenth century. It consisted largely of downtrodden, poverty-stricken peasants and workers with a standard of living bordering on starvation. There was a small class of industrial workers, somewhat better off than the peasant masses; a relatively small, comfortably situated middle-class; and a still smaller wealthy class, made up chiefly of landlords who owned much of the land and controlled much of the industry. Among the masses, the Jews undoubtedly led the most precarious life. They were forced to concentrate in the towns and cities where their opportunities of earning a living were hampered by all kinds of discriminatory laws and regulations. "I can certify," states a thorough student of the Eastern European Jews in the latter part of the nineteenth century, "that nothing in Europe is so poor, no beings earn their crust of rye bread with such bitterness as nine-tenths of the Russian Jews." [1] And another impartial observer, [2] writing in 1892, states that only a very small minority of the Russian Jews possess any certain means of existence. "As to the masses," he writes, "they possess nothing; and they are far poorer than the Christian populace, who at any rate own some land."

The Jews in Russia proper were permitted to live only in certain regions, the so-called Pale of Settlement, and excluded from others. Few lived in rural communities, the great bulk being crowded into compact sections of towns and cities. Only about 15 per cent of the Russian and Polish Jews had a definite trade, 13.2 per cent being artisans, mainly tailors and bootmakers, and about 2 per cent industrial workers.[3] Catering chiefly to their co-religionists, the artisans eked out a living with great difficulty, leading a hand-to-mouth existence that often compelled them to seek aid from charity. The industrial workers were hardly better off, as the wages received were insufficient to take care of their good-sized families.

The great majority of the Russian Jews were shopkeepers and petty merchants who went into business for lack of other opportunities. Retailing their meager stock in groschen in ramshackle buildings surrounding the marketplace, on stands improvised every morning, or on push carts, these "storekeepers" were even worse off economically than the artisans. The business done by the "merchants" was confined mainly to buying the products of the peasant or landlord and reselling them in wholesale or retail — a task involving hard mental as well as physical work, since it was conducted in a very primitive manner and resulted in earnings often insufficient for a meager existence. Contrary to the conception prevalent, even in our own country, the retailer and even the wholesale distributor of goods is really performing a task essential to the normal functioning of society. This has become increasingly clear even in Soviet Russia where the "bourgeois businessman" has been most hated. Nevertheless, the Jew who has been forced into the position of dispenser of goods was looked upon as one who lived off the fat of the land without contributing to it.

A large percentage of the Russian and Polish Jews in the smaller towns had no fixed occupations. These were the so-called *Luftmenschen* (people living on air). Shopkeeper one day, broker another, clerk at one time and tutor at another, this *Luftmensch* seldom knew whence his and his family's next meal was coming. Nowhere is such an occupationless Jew depicted more graphically than in the works of *"Mendele Moher Seforim."* One such description is worth translating in full:

> If, for instance, a Jew of Turnejadevka should suddenly be
> asked: "How do you provide for yourself and your family?"
> he will at first stare at you incomprehensibly and be at a

loss as to what to say. When he will have recovered somewhat from his astonishment, he will reply naively:

"Who, I? How I am making a living? Well, well. There is a God, I tell you; there is a God who does not forsake any one of his creatures. He is providing at present and undoubtedly will do so in the future. I tell you there is no doubt about it."

"Still, what do you do for a living? Have you a profession or trade?"

"Praised be the Lord! As you see me, I possess, blessed be the Name, a gift from Him, a singing voice; I chant the prayers on the High Holy Days in this vicinity; I am a circumcision expert, and as a *Matzah* perforator I stand alone in the entire world; at times I manage to do a little matchmaking. As you see me, I have a pew in the synagogue And then, between you and me, I am the owner of a *shenkel* (little saloon). I have also a goat that yields some milk once in a while, and not far from here I have a well-to-do relative who can also be milked when times become bad..."[4]

Despite all of his professions and possessions and despite his supreme confidence in the Lord and reliance upon his "wealthy" kin, this Jewish jack-of-all-trades led a most miserable existence. His large family was housed in one or two crudely furnished rooms. His daily meal consisted of a milkless, meatless barley soup *(krupnik)*. Once a week, on the Sabbath, if luck was with him, he managed to have meat at his table which his wife shredded into tiny pieces so that everyone of his numerous children could have a taste of this delicacy. Clothes were worn threadbare, and only once in several years could he afford new clothes for himself or his family.

In Galicia and Rumania, the other two lands whence the Stamford Jews or their parents came originally, conditions resembled closely those described above. In Galicia it was mainly the natural poverty and backwardness of the country, and in Rumania the discriminatory laws that made the existence of the Jews most precarious. In each of these countries there were some well-situated and even wealthy Jews but those were few in number and, as a rule, never felt the need for emigrating.

Although they were undoubtedly on a higher cultural level than the illiterate peasants who surrounded them, the Jewish masses of eastern Europe nevertheless led a life regulated by a code of laws which not only tended to keep them apart from the rest of the population but which ordered minutely their every-day life. Since adherence to that code was the rule, it meant that they were obliged to observe scrupulously a myriad of regulations and commands directing every phase of their life from the cradle to the grave.

The training for this kind of circumscribed life began very early. No sooner did a child reach the age of four, often only three, than he was wrapped up in a prayer shawl *(talit),* and carried away to the religious school *(heder).* There he was left to the mercy of a teacher *(melamed),* who, as a rule, lacked all training, to be introduced to the intricate system of Hebrew reading. The school consisted of a single room which also served as a kitchen, dining room and bedroom for the entire family of the teacher. Here together with a score or more other children the child spent most of the day and, upon reaching the "mature" age of seven or eight, much of the evening. At the age of five or six he was introduced to the Old Testament in Hebrew and two or three years later to the Talmud written in Aramaic. By the time he reached thirteen, if his education had not been interrupted and his mind was good, he was expected to be able to continue his study of the Talmud by himself.

The Jewish child had little or no contact with his non-Jewish neighbor, and this developed all kinds of prejudices in the minds of both, prejudices which were carefully fostered and encouraged by their respective parents. In more enlightened Galicia the Jewish children were compelled by law to attend in the mornings a public school for at least three years. Many of them managed to keep out of it, but even if they did attend they remained quite segregated from the Gentile children, as the schools they attended were very often institutions especially designed for them, and subsidized by the philanthropist Baron de Hirsch. In Russia and Rumania the child was not even obliged to attend a school of this sort, but at best learned a smattering of the predominant language of the country by means of private Jewish tutors.

Separated from the rest of the population the child grew into manhood or womanhood knowing only one world — that of his own group, which was governed by the strict code of laws of the Jewish religion. As already intimated, this religion did not confine itself to special occasions, like holidays and fast days. It dominated virtually every moment of the individual's waking life and penetrated, so to speak, into every nook and corner of his abode. Even in his sleep a Jew had to guard against the displacement of the skull-cap which he was obliged to wear at all times.

There was a rule for every physical and mental function a Jew performed. Infringement of any one of the multitude of regulations was sure to result in punishment in the future world as well as active disapproval from neighbors.

Nevertheless, it would be a mistake to assume that this rigid discipline allowed for little joy of living, that it resulted in but a monastic way of life. As a matter of fact, the necessarily drab everyday existence was pleasantly interrupted by holidays and family celebrations which were part of this very system of life. It was these holidays and celebrations, occurring at regular and frequent intervals, which, as Heine in his poem *"Princess Sabbath"* describes, changed like by magic, the Jewish home from a shack into a palace and the poor hard-working Jew into a prince. On such occasions the Jew would find joy and happiness in the company of his fellows in the synagogue and particularly in the midst of his family whose life was characterized by extraordinary cohesion, warmth and devotion.

Obedience to the law was not by any means restricted to the observance of religious precepts but required a devotion to learning, to scholarship. Few societies or groups took such a serious view of education as the Jews. Mothers sang in their lullabies of Torah being the highest of goods. To educate their children parents would shun no sacrifice. The day on which the child formally started his studies was marked by a big family celebration, as was his advancement to the study of the Bible. Scholarship was looked up to and respected as no other accomplishment; the learned were considered the real aristocrats. Students of promise were willingly supported by the members of the community.

Another very important characteristic of Jewish group life was charitableness. Dependent as they usually were upon themselves, the Jews have developed a strong sense of pity for the destitute. Even the poor man deemed it his duty to invite the more unfortunate to his table and to share with him the hard-earned meal. The destitute and helpless were not, however, left to the mercy of the individual, but cared for in a systematic way by the Jewish community as a whole through its various organizations and institutions created for that purpose. In view of the fact that many of the institutions maintained at present by the Jews of Stamford as elsewhere in this country are replicas of those found in the old country, a brief description of the system of poor relief developed by the Jewish communities of Europe will not be amiss here.

The support of the poor and otherwise helpless was all along considered by the Jews as an obligation rather than a benevolent act. The Hebrew term *tsedakah* (righteousness) used for charity by Jews everywhere is therefore far from accidental. Whether resident or stranger, every needy individual was taken care of in one manner of another by the community, rather than left to become a public charge. Already in Talmudic times Jewish communities maintained a charity box *(kuppah)* to which every resident was required to contribute regularly, and out of which the indigent were paid every Friday an amount sufficient for fourteen meals. Often a charity bowl *(tamhoi)* to which members of the community donated food articles for immediate relief of the hungry was also part of the charity system. Even residence of only thirty days obligated one to contribute to the kuppah.

The system of charity maintained by the Jewish communities from the early Middle Ages down to recent times included (1) feeding the hungry (2) clothing the naked (3) visiting the sick (4) burying the dead and comforting the mourners (5) redeeming the captive (6) educating the fatherless and sheltering the homeless and (7) providing poor maidens with dowries. These objectives were usually carried out by individual societies corresponding to each of the above-named branches. In some cases institutions having their own buildings were created. Thus every good-sized community had a home for the needy aged and sick, the *hekdesh,* which also accommodated the destitute stranger. The homes for the aged maintained by contemporary Jewish communities in America are a direct outgrowth of this institution, while the orphanages and schools *(Talmud Torahs)* are but a continuation of similar institutions in European Jewish communities. A host of other endeavers found in presentday American Jewish communities have their roots in Old World Jewish life. Particularly worthy of note among these are the *Gemilat Hesed,* or free loan, societies encountered in practically every American Jewish community, the underlying principle of which is that the best aid that can be given to the poor is to help him to help himself.

Immersed in his own group, the Jew, like the neighbors among whom he lived, showed little concern with what was going on outside his own narrow circle. He spoke his own language, and of the language of the country he knew just enough to get by, with the help of gestures, in his business deals. All of his activities took place within his own group, and the little contact he did have with Gentiles was of an impersonal nature and limited to relationships of an economic character. Assimilation, as far as the masses were concerned, was well nigh impossible as it meant absorption by force. Forceful attempts at assimilating Jews, particularly at converting them, as the government of Tsar Nicholas I attempted to do, never met with success. They only served to strengthen the ties binding the individual to his religion and culture. Furthermore, in most localities assimilation would have meant becoming absorbed into a group of people on a much lower cultural level, the illiterate peasants and villagers. The Jews, therefore, resisted those attempts with every means at their disposal, and remained segregated from the rest of the population.

There was, of course, an element that tried, and at times even succeeded, in becoming assimilated into the dominant group. But this element was extremely small and limited to well-to-do businessmen and professionals living in the larger towns. The large masses of the people, as pointed out above were not affected by this tendency on the part of their wealthy brethren and openly and actively showed the greatest contempt for the "assimilationists," as they were called.

What the masses of people did was to turn increasingly to certain movements which had the effect of sublimating and hence of making their lot somewhat easier to bear and their outlook more hopeful. The first of these was Hasidism, a doctrine steeped in mysticism and teaching that God can best be served through joy. Since it minimized and even affected to look down upon learning and the rigidity of the code of laws and, on the other hand, assured even the ignorant and the lowly of the possibility of communicating with his God in any language and in any manner, it had an irresistible appeal to the common man. In the period under consideration, Hasidism, whose leaders and interpreters were the wonder rabbis *(Tsadikkim),* included among its adherents hundreds of thousands of individuals who found consolation in its simple doctrine.

The less mystically inclined became adherents of the *Haskalah* (enlightenment), a movement propagated by Moses Mendelssohn in the latter half of the eighteenth century among the Jews of Germany and transplanted to Eastern Europe. This movement, limited to a select group, made the acquisition of Western culture by the Jews its chief aim, in the belief that in doing so the Jewish problem would thus be solved. Since it also advocated that the Jew rid himself of his peculiar clothes and other marks distinguishing him from the rest of the population, the *Haskalah* may be looked up as a sort of vague assimilationist, or rather imitationist, movement. Although its appeal was much more limited than that of Hasidism, it nevertheless managed to produce in many a Jewish community good-sized groups of individuals who acquired a knowledge of German— the symbol of Western culture — and other European languages and who displayed an almost pathological love for the classic literature and learning in general. The leaders of the *Haskalah* mostly used the Hebrew language as a medium for propagating their ideas and doctrines. As a result, the ancient tongue of the Jews received a new lease on life, eventually developing into the modern, living language it is today. *Haskalah* writers imitated western forms of literature in Hebrew, drawing their themes from ancient and modern Jewish life, and thus laid the foundation of a modern Hebrew literature. The *Haskalah* thus prepared the ground for modern Jewish nationalism. That, to some extent, the "enlightenment" movement may even be considered as the forerunner of political Zionism can be seen from the fact that the first adherents of modern Zionism were drawn primarily from the ranks of the maskilim, as the followers of the *Haskalah* were known.

While offering some consolation, these movements failed, of course, to solve the actual problems faced by the masses of the people. *Haskalah* did not seem to fulfill the promises it held out. The inspiration received by many from following the teachings of Hasidism made the trials and tribulations just a bit easier to bear. With the rise of nationalistic feeling throughout Europe, the Jew sought salvation in a nationalism of his own — Zionism, which made its appearance at about that time in the form of a semi-utopian scheme called Hovevei-Zionism. This national awakening was, to be sure, the result of the general nationalistic stir felt among the neighboring ethnic groups, but it was greatly stimulated by the waves of pogroms and oppressive measures to which the Jews became increasingly exposed. This brings us to the second major factor responsible for Jewish emigration, namely, persecution.

The Jews of tsaristic Russia were always the victims of discrimination and oppression. Each tsar who ascended the throne in the nineteenth century found some new method, devised some new plan to "protect" Holy Russia from its millions of "infidels." While the early rulers and their henchmen were satisfied with passing one discriminatory law after another, designed to make the life of the Jew more and more miserable, those of the later years embarked upon a policy of cruel extermination, known as the pogrom. During the reign of Alexander III (1881-1894), literally hundreds of Jewish communities were devastated and thousands of Jews massacred or maimed. Jewish women were assaulted under the very eyes of their husbands, and Jewish children were torn limb from limb while their parents were forced to look on. The helplessness and utter despair of the Jews is apparent from the following description of a protest meeting held by the Jewish congregation in St. Petersburg in 1882:

> When the preacher — an eye witness relates — began to picture in a broken voice the present position of Jewry, one long moan, coming, as it were, from one breast, suddenly burst forth and filled the synagogue. Everybody wept, the old, the young, the long robed paupers, the elegant dandies dressed in latest fashion, the men in government service, the physicians, the students, not to speak of the women. For two or three minutes did these heart-rending moans resound — this cry of common sorrow which had issued from the Jewish heart. The rabbi was unable to continue. He stood upon the pulpit, covered his eyes with his hands, and wept like a child. [5]

One of the high points in these atrocities was reached in the pogroms of Kishinef and Homel in 1903-04, during the reign of the last of the tsars, Nicholas II. So savage and ruthless was the Kishinef massacre that it called forth expressions of indignation throughout the civilized world and an official protest from the United States. Coming as they did at a time when the gates of America were wide open and its reputation as a land of unlimited opportunities widely circulated, these outrages marked the beginning of a wave of Jewish emigration that did not halt, excepting during the World War, until, in 1921, the doors of the United States were tightly shut.

Since what is usually referred to as Poland proper was incorporated into the Russian empire toward the end of the 18th century, the Jews living there were exposed to approximately the same treatment as their Russian coreligionists. In Galicia, the section of Poland that became, at about the same time, part of the Austro-Hungarian empire, the Jews, to be sure, suffered no large-scale physical attacks, but were exposed to all kinds of discrimination which, combined with the the natural poverty and over-population of the country, made their lot a very sad one. In Rumania, a rampant anti-Semitism, planned and carried on under the auspices of the government, progressively reduced the civil rights of the Jews. No fewer than 65 legislative acts, all designed to curb the rights of the Jews, were passed by the government. "The history of Rumanian legislation against the Jews during the nineteenth century," states one source, "is one of the most remarkable in all the annals of Jewish persecution. It culminated in the Artisan Bill of March 16, 1902, which was intended to prevent Jews from earning their livelihood by any form of handicraft or trade..."[6]

Maltreated and denied what we have learned to consider elementary human rights, living the life of an outcast and deprived of earning a livelihood, the Eastern European Jew took to emigrating to "the land of opportunity" as the only hope of salvation. Slow in the beginning, the stream of emigration grew into ever larger proportions, so that whole villages and towns were emptied of their Jewish inhabitants, and every ship anchoring in New York harbor discharged scores, at times hundreds, of Jews on the friendly shores of America. Included among these were the present-day Stamford Jews or their parents.

Footnotes

1. Leroy-Beaulieu, quoted by A. Ruppin, The Jews of To-Day, p.57
2. Errea, L. "Le Juifs Russes," Journal du Nord, 1892, pp.120-121
3. Jewish Encyclopedia, X 534-36
4. Mendele Moher Seforim (S.J.Abramowitz). Travels of Benjamin III (Yiddish), p.9
5. Dubnow, S.M. History of the Jews in Russia and Poland, Vol.II, p.286
6. Jewish Encyclopedia, Vol. X, p.516

CHAPTER III

EARLY ARRIVALS

Although Jews could be found in several towns of Connecticut even in Colonial times, there is no indication of their having settled in Stamford prior to the middle of the past century.[1] {1}The Jewish settlers of those early days, who were of Spanish-Portuguese origin and came here after a sojourn in the West Indies, left hardly a trace behind them in Connecticut, since they either were absorbed into the native population or left for other parts of the country.{2} In the late 1840's, Jewish immigrants from Germany, drifting in mainly from New York together with their German compatriots, began laying the foundations of prosperous settlements, particularly in New Haven and Hartford. These Jews did not find their way to Stamford until 1859, when one of them established himself there with his family. This first Jewish family was soon joined by two other German-Jewish families, and in the 1880's three other families, two of German origin and one of Dutch arrived.{3} This was practically the full extent to which West-European Jews settled in the town, except for recent years when several German and Austrian Jewish families, fleeing from Nazi Germany, found refuge in Stamford. Of these six families only one remains, the others having left Stamford at the beginning of this century or earlier.

The earliest Jewish settlers of Stamford consisted, as far as can be traced, of three families of German origin, namely the Foxes, the Cohens and the Bernhards. In the Stamford Register of Electors for 1860 Jacob Fox appears as an elector admitted in that year. Since the prerequisites for becoming an elector were at least two years' residence in the State and six months in the particular town, Jacob Fox must have come to Connecticut at least

Tobias Bernhard (1841–1914) seated on the left, in front of his Dry Goods & Millinery store at 123 Main St. (later 300 block). Founded 1868. President, Stamford Board of Trade, and prominent real estate owner.

by 1858 and settled in Stamford by 1859. As no trace can be found of any Jew residing in Stamford prior to this date, he can safely be considered the first Jewish settler of Stamford.

Jacob Fox was later joined by three other relatives (their exact relationship is unknown) the brothers Isaac, Peter, and Charles Fox. The first mention of Isaac is in connection with a birth registered in 1871 in the Town Register, and that of the other two occurs in the city directory of 1890.{4} At least two of these four individuals were married and living with their families, as the Register records the birth of sons to Jacob and Esther Fox and Isaac Fox and Bertha Miller on May 16, 1863 and February 25, 1871, respectively.

The records also show that the Cohens arrived in 1862 and the Bernhards in 1867. Wolff Cohen, who advertises his clothing store in the Stamford Advocate of September 26, 1862 and is admitted as an elector on March 28, 1864, appears to have been the first of the Cohen family that settled in Stamford at that time. With him were his wife Harriet, and Rachel and Henry his children.{5} Others included Samuel H. Cohen and his wife Kitty, and Samuel Cohen.{6,7} Records show that Samuel H. was admitted as an elector on March 22 and Samuel on March 27, 1875. Of the Bernhards, there were Tobias, his wife Annie Benjamin, a son Solomon, born in Stamford May 21, 1871, and his brother Henry, who married Rachel Cohen in Stamford on January 25, 1871.

Thus we find that as late as the 1870's the total Jewish population of Stamford consisted of little more than a score of individuals belonging to three families.{8} As intimated above, they were all from Germany, but did not come to Stamford directly from that country.{9} They appear to have been quite thoroughly acculturated by the time they reached Stamford, for they did not seen to mind being detached from a Jewish environment, the only time they evinced a desire for contact with a Jewish community being in moments of crises, like birth, marriage and death. But such a situation seems to have been taken care of satisfactorily simply by the bringing of a rabbi of the Reform Temple from New York, as was done in the case of the marriage of Henry Bernhard and Rachel Cohen.{10} One old-time Jewish resident recalls these families as keeping aloof from the more recently arrived immigrants. That they showed no interest in things Jewish is further evidenced by the fact that their names fail to appear on any of the early documents and records relating to the founding of the various Jewish communal institutions by a handful of poor

Eastern-European newcomers at a time when they were well established and prosperous citizens.{11}

Unlike the later arrivals from Russia and Poland, these early settlers did not enter Stamford through the back door, poor, unable to speak the language of the country, and ignorant of American ways. They came here as Americanized individuals with adequate means to establish themselves at once in their chosen occupations. No sooner did Jacob Fox arrive than he opened, in 1859, a tailoring shop which he shortly afterwards expanded into an important clothing store.[2] Isaac became the owner of a saloon on Main Street to which he later added a billiard parlor, and Peter and Charles followed him into the same business by establishing a saloon on Gay Street which became very popular.

Wolff Cohen, like Jacob Fox, became a merchant tailor, who employed "three hands" in 1862.[3] An advertisement appearing in the Stamford Advocate of September 26, 1862, announces that his "Stamford Clothing Establishment" at the Union Hotel "has a large assortment of clothes and cassimeres, vestings, etc., which he will make up to order at the lowest cash prices and warranted to fit," as well as "a large assortment of ready made clothing." Samuel Cohen and Kitty, wife of Samuel H., are listed in the 1879 city directory as owners of a "fancy goods and millinery" shop on Atlantic Street, opposite Central Park, which in 1881 was located on 7 Park Row.{12} Samuel H. Cohen on the other hand, established himself as a lawyer in Hubbard's Block, Main Street and in 1876 served for a period of six months as judge of the probate court.[4]

Tobias Bernhard, who "for four years previously had conducted stores in Danbury, Waterbury and Bridgeport" soon after his arrival in 1867, established, in partnership with his brother, the "New York Fancy Store" at No.5 Seely's Block.[5] The "grand opening" of the shop is announced in the Stamford Advocate issue of March 20, 1868, and, as is evident from the variety of different articles advertised for sale, it could probably lay claim to being a real department store. Aside from this, Tobias Bernhard is also referred to as a large real estate owner and as one who has "helped organize the Board of Trade of which he is an active director."[6]

That these early settlers arrived in Stamford at an early age is brought out in several items recorded in the Town Hall Registers on the occasion of birth and marriage. Thus, at the birth of a son Jacob, on May 16, 1863, both Isaac Fox and his wife are recorded as being 26 years of age.{13} Wolff Cohen was 40 years old and his wife 33 when their son Henry was born on March 31, 1865.{14} Tobias Bernhard was 30 years old and his wife 21 when their son Solomon was born on May 31, 1871, and his brother Henry was 25 and his bride 20 when they were married on January 25 of the same year.

These families remained in Stamford only long enough to witness the coming of the first Jewish immigrants from Eastern Europe. The Foxes as well as the Cohens had disappeared from the Stamford scene by the turn of the century, without leaving a trace behind them.{15} Of the Bernhards, only a son and a grandson of Tobias remain in Stamford, the other brother, Henry and his wife having left town soon after their wedding.{16} Since these early settlers contributed practically nothing toward the laying of the foundations of Jewish community life in Stamford, they can hardly be considered as pioneers of the settlement. They were merely precursors of the actual builders of the community who began arriving from Russia and Poland in the late eighties.{17} Before embarking upon an account of these latter, however, let us take a glance at Stamford in those years — to acquaint ourselves with the environment into which these harbingers of ever larger groups of Jewish settlers came.

Footnotes
1. Those towns were: Hartford, New Haven, Guilford, Branford, Middletown, Stratford, Fairfield, Norwalk and Danbury. Nearby Norwalk harbored for a number of years a Jewish congregation which had fled British rule in New York, under the leadership of their rabbi, Gershom Seixas, during the Revolution.{18} (Leon Huhner, "The Jews of New England" in Publications of the American Jewish Historical Society, XI, 87-94).
2. Huntington, E.B. History of Stamford, p.474.
3. Huntington, E.B. History of Stamford, p.474
4. Stamford Advocate, July 7, 1876.
5. Gillespie, E.T. Picturesque Stamford, p. 279
6. Gillespie, E.T. Picturesque Stamford, p. 279

CHAPTER IV

THE TOWN THE SETTLERS FOUND

Stamford in the eighties was a town of about 15,000 inhabitants, which had not yet lost its country-like aspect. Its old Meeting-House had long ago disappeared, the modern Town Hall, erected across the street from its site, taking its place. But there remained in its stead the "Green," typical of the New England town. Its streets, principal avenues and thoroughfares were lined with "magnificent and stately shade trees." The trading center consisting, according to a contemporary account, of "many handsome business blocks on which substantial new brick buildings with plate glass show windows displaying up-to-the-minute articles of clothing, furnishings and novelties," had replaced the old frame structures. The Boston Post Road stage had given way to the twenty-five daily trains and the several steamers connecting the town with the metropolis. Modern conveniences had begun to spread. A water system had been in existence for some time. Electricity had just begun to displace gas and oil as a means for lighting the streets and homes, and the telephone had been gaining in public booths and private subscribers.

Stamford was already something of an industrial center. Farmers were still numerous in the surrounding country, but the majority of the town's inhabitants derived their livelihood, directly or indirectly, from industry. The Yale and Towne lock factory already employed 650 workers. Other industrial establishments, manufacturing hardware, carriages, furniture, hats, shoes, etc., provided work for additional hundreds and the laying of the parallel railroad lines for many more.

The town had been brought into much closer contact with New York by the increased facilities of communication. Hundreds of commuters made daily trips to and from New York. Newspapers appeared on the stands, and social life generally was brought within the orbit of cosmopolitan life. Thus, while traveling companies were still delighting large audiences with "mammoth" spectacles on the Tailboard stage of a van on a corner of Pacific Street, featuring "twenty-six artists and a band of genuine Sioux including the great Red Cloud's niece and nephew," while the Stamford Club House satisfied crowds of Stamfordites with its performance of "Soiree' d'Ethiope," and another local society entertained its audiences with its presentation of "Orpheus and Eurydice," many a Stamfordite showed a definite preference for the more urbane Broadway show. The New York, New Haven and Hartford Railroad ran a special theatre train every week to New York. Exclusive organizations, such as the Stamford Yacht Club, Lawn Tennis Club, Angler's Club, Rod and Gun Club, etc., further testify to Stamford's sophistication.

The average Stamford citizen indulged in driving and horseback riding, in ice skating, roller skating, and cycling which had begun to become fads, joined clubs and societies, and frequented the ever popular drinking places. The latter, if not entirely a creation of the German residents, were certainly popularized by them. Music also owed its local development to the Germans, whose societies were forever giving concerts and song recitals. The Stamford Glee Club, Vocal Society and Oratorio Society were results of their efforts. Dropping in for a drink and a chat at the Germania Beer Garden or similar places and attending a song recital or concert were social customs prevalent at the time.

Educationally, too, Stamford was well advanced, considering its size and the period. Aside from the dozen or so excellent private preparatory schools, some of which enjoyed a wide reputation, there existed a progressive public school system comprising a number of grade schools and a high school to which the less wealthy sent their children to be instructed. There were also a business college offering courses in stenography, commercial penmanship, German, telegraphy and architecture, a public library, and other educational facilities.

Stamford already in those days showed signs of becoming a cosmopolitan city. Among those of foreign birth or parentage Irish, Germans and English were the most numerous numbering in 1879, 857, 161, and 117 families, respectively.{19} Only 42 families were Scotch, 31 Scandinavian, 19 Italian, 4 Swiss, 8 French, 3 Polish, 2 Welsh and 5 of other origin.[1]

Approximately 200 Negroes added to the diversity of the town's population.

With the exception of the Irish and Germans, none of the groups numerically prominent in Stamford today, namely, the Italians, Jews and Poles, gave the slightest indication in the eighties of becoming important elements in the town's population. The Irish and Germans, on the other hand, were by that time quite firmly established in the community, many of them taking prominent parts in the commercial, industrial and professional life of the town. Indeed, certain trades were practically monopolized by them. Thus the bakeries, saloons and barber shops were largely in the hands of Germans, while certain types of factory work, civil service, cab driving, and even gardening were mostly in the hands of the Irish. The latter concentrated in a particular section of the town known till today as "Dublin." Another section was known as "Algiers," because of its preponderantly Negro population.

In the eighties Stamford was an almost completely English-speaking, largely native community, with a marked social class system and a rather sophisticated way of life. Native institutions and customs predominated, although the Irish and Germans had their institutions firmly established and were making themselves felt in the economic, social and cultural life of the community. The prejudice that once existed against the Irish had largely worn off, but ill feeling against foreigners, from which the former immigrants themselves were by no means free, still existed in the native community.[2] This in brief, is what Stamford looked like when the East European Jewish immigrant discovered it.

Footnotes

1. These figures are taken from the report of the Connecticut Bible Society conducted in 1888 and printed in the Stamford Advocate of July 13, 1888.
2. The Italians, for instance, who were very few in number at the time are on several occasions severely condemned in the local press. The Stamford Advocate of May 16, 1884, refers to them as "untamed Italians" because of their "chasing some young girls across the fields" and threatens them with "war" unless they change their tactics, and the Stamford Herald of April 25, 1883, states that "the stealing and lying capacities of the Italian rag-pickers which frequent the dooryards are well known."

CHAPTER V

LAYING THE FOUNDATIONS

The pioneers of the Stamford Jewish settlement came largely from the provinces of pre-war Russia, particularly Lithuania, White Russia, Poland and Latvia. None of them came directly from Europe, and very few brought their families with them. Of the American cities that had provided homes for them prior to their settling in Stamford, New York came first, but towns as far west as Toledo, Ohio, and Kansas City, Missouri, were among the localities in which they had sojourned.

They usually arrived from New York City and stayed only long enough to dispose of the wares which they were peddling, returning "home" as soon as this was done. It was only after a number of such visits that some of them decided to settle. For an explanation of this rather unusual way of finding a permanent home, we must turn to the position in which those individuals found themselves as well as to conditions prevalent at the time.

New York was the mecca of the Jewish immigrant. As already intimated, many of those who succeeded in escaping from Tsarist Russia, starving Galicia, or Rumania, came to America without a trade or profession. Having had some experience in buying and selling, they naturally turned to peddling as a means of earning a livelihood. All one needed to become a full-fledged merchant of this sort was a few dollars to buy some goods — any kind of goods that lent themselves to being carried in a pack, the knowledge of a few English words, a resounding voice, and above all a sturdy pair of legs and a strong back. The stock in trade covered a variety of articles, notions, clothing, particularly women's wear, and tinware being the most common. Those owning horse-and-wagon outfits often included junk in their merchandise, some dealing in it exclusively. New York, of course, provided ample opportunity for such aspiring businessmen, but competition was too keen, much keener at any rate than in the "country," where the possibilities seemed unlimited. Connecticut had a particular attraction for these individuals. It had scores of towns in close proximity — towns large enough to have an abundance of customers, yet small enough not to have too many stores. And what with the small villages and farming communities surrounding those towns, many an enterprising "merchant" took to the road leading to Connecticut. Travelling from town to town by trolley or directly by boat, he arrived in Stamford, which in time came to be considered a convenient point from which the surrounding territory could be canvassed or further penetration into the interior of the State undertaken.[1] After repeated returns and sojourns, some of these itinerant traders decided to remain in Stamford, either continuing to ply their trade and eventually opening small shops of their own, or finding jobs in factories or other establishments.

The first of the East-European Jews to arrive in Stamford via the peddlers' route was Jacob Rosenblum. The exact date of his arrival is hard to determine, but it was about 1880 or 1881. Born in Wilki, Lithuania, he left his homeland to escape being drafted into military service in the Tsar's army. Upon his arrival in this country, he joined a relative living in Pennsylvania, but after a while he left for New York City whence he peddled his way into Stamford. In the old country his father was a barrel maker, but he himself came here without the knowledge of a trade, and hence took to junk peddling. In Stamford he continued in this occupation, doing odd jobs in slack times. The two settlers who arrived shortly afterwards, Abraham Cohen and Joseph Nachemson, came to Stamford with their families as well as with trades, the first being a shoemaker and the second a tailor.{20} These two families also came to Stamford after spending some time in one or more other places in the United States. To supplement their earnings, both families turned their homes into boarding houses for itinerant peddlers and for single men who had settled down in Stamford.

The year of the great blizzard, 1888, has come to be looked upon by the pioneers of the Stamford Jewish community as a chronological starting point from which all past events are reckoned. Happenings long past have occurred either a few years before or after that catastrophe. The eight years intervening between 1880 and the blizzard are considered a sort of prehistoric period, or at least a time when individual, detached Jews were roaming the streets and alleys of Stamford, uncertain as to whether they would be able to find any permanent abodes for themselves and their yet unborn families, and doubting whether this city of Yankees and Irish could ever give birth to a Jewish community.

The formative period of the Stamford Jewish community, namely, 1880-1903, divides itself into two parts. The first, 1880-1888, is characterized by a rather chaotic attempt on the part of a handful of bewildered individuals to adjust themselves to a not altogether friendly environment. All of their energy and time are consumed in eking out a living, and moments in which they can turn their minds to other things are rare. This antediluvian period added but few new Jewish settlers: a young man, originally from Bialystok, who opened a clothing shop and kept aloof from the "peddlers"; two young men, one hailing from Witebsk, White Russia, and the other from a small town in Lithuania, who arrived two years before the blizzard and embarked upon a career of extensive peddling; and one born in another Lithuanian village, who arrived a year before the storm and while taking to peddling like the rest, succeeded in amassing wealth and laying the foundations of a considerable family fortune. If to these are added three brothers, originally also Wilki, Lithuania, who came a year before the blizzard and established themselves as junk peddler, shoemaker, and dry goods dealer, respectively, and an extremely pious young man, hailing from another Lithuanian village, who came to Stamford, narrowly escaping the blizzard on his way, and started peddling tinware, the group which was eventually to constitute the nucleus of the Stamford Jewish community is complete.{21}

The second part, 1889-1903 can be described as a period in which the preliminary ground-work for a distinct community was laid. In the course of these fifteen years the lot of many improved considerably; some of the group became quite well adjusted, and some even succeeded in establishing themselves firmly economically as well as socially. No sooner did this happen than a wealth of energy and enthusiasm was let loose — all directed toward creating conditions under which Jewish group life could be perpetuated.

Who were the individuals who came to Stamford between 1880 and 1888? How did they live and conduct their affairs? As the place of origin Lithuania figures most prominently. Of the localities in Lithuania the town of Wilki comes first. With the exception of two or three, they were all unmarried young people with something of the adventurer in them. Coming from one of the culturally as well as economically most backward regions of Russia and from the lower middle class or proletariat, they brought with them little education. None of them, however, was illiterate, as all were able to read the Hebrew of the prayer book, and some had a fair knowledge of the Talmud and the Old Testament. Some, too, were products of the *Haskalah* (enlightenment) and nationalist movements, and, hence, had some knowledge of German and a smattering of general culture. Their experience in this country prior to their coming to Stamford had broadened their view of things somewhat; they no longer were as pious as when they left their homeland, but the beliefs and practices of their orthodox faith still permeated their lives and determined their actions. The concessions they were forced to make to changed conditions, however, resulted in a state where the old practices and beliefs were adhered to only when convenient or possible. Thus, most of them worked on Saturdays, had their beards shaved off, and were not very strict about their daily prayers — all serious violations of orthodox religion. This, however, did not mean that they were intent upon becoming assimilated, that they were anxious to throw overboard their cultural heritage. On the contrary, no group showed a greater desire to adhere to its folkways and mores, to transplant and perpetuate its culture than these people.

Upon their arrival in Stamford and for some time afterwards, these individuals boarded with one of the four Jewish families who took boarders. These boarding houses were located on Canal Street, on Pacific Street, and opposite the old Railroad Station — predominantly Irish neighborhoods, bordering on the business center of the town. No special provision was made by those households to accommodate their boarders or guests. Furniture was scanty, with hardly enough beds for the family, but there was plenty of floor space on which to put mattresses. A bed of this sort and breakfast cost the boarder fifteen cents. Another "hotel" charged twenty cents, but this included a regular bed and a glass of tea before retiring, in addition to a reading from the German classics by the host who claimed to be well versed in them.

Dietary laws were still observed by these transient settlers. As no kosher meat or bread was obtainable in Stamford, it had to be brought from New York or from Port Chester, which already had an organized Jewish community. These foods were usually transported by individuals returning from New York or sent by messenger. Religious services were also arranged for, although with difficulty. A *Sefer Torah* (Holy Scroll), indispensable to an organized service, had been acquired upon making a small down-payment, and on some Saturdays it was found possible to assemble ten adults — the minimum required for conducting a service — in one of the boarding houses and, before an improvised altar and with one of their number acting as reader, pray to the Lord in accordance with custom.

The years immediately following the blizzard of 1888 witnessed a more rapid growth of the Jewish population. Single men got married, and those who came leaving families and relatives behind were gradually joined by the latter. Former peddlers who succeeded in accumulating some capital established themselves as proprietors of small shops or, if unsuccessful in their enterprise, as employees in stores and factories. Several of those who arrived at this period brought with them some previous American business experience as well as sufficient money to open shops or to take over previously existing ones, without having first to trudge the streets or roam the countryside with packs on their backs.

It was in 1889 that the first attempt at communal organization was made. In July of that year, on the occasion of completing the payments on the Holy Scroll, twenty-two persons gathered and formally constituted themselves a congregation. Some of them were transients who, because of frequent sojourns in Stamford, were interested in promoting regular services. The Articles of Incorporation recorded by the Town Clerk on September 7, 1889, stipulate that the congregation be known as Agudath Sholom, Society of Peace, or, as the authors of the document erroneously translated it, Knot of Peace, and that "the valuables of this congregation is only for Stamford, Connecticut, defined, and shall not be never removed from here." This would seem to indicate that the group had confidence in the growth and development of the congregation despite the skepticism expressed in a clause which provided for the transfer of the Torah back to New York in case the congregation was reduced to less than five.

Burial in a Jewish cemetery in accordance with Jewish custom and tradition is considered of utmost importance by the orthodox Jews. Custom also requires that the deceased be buried within twenty-four hours after death. Although the members of the group were all comparatively young, the fear of meeting with sudden death and of being buried in unconsecrated soil was ever present. Thus, we find this handful of people setting as their next task the buying of a cemetery of their own. Two years after organizing the congregation, on August 21, 1891, when the permanence of the settlement seemed assured, the Articles of Association of the Agoodat Solima Cemetery Association were drawn up and signed.[2] Only a month later, on September 2, a deed, showing the purchase of a tract of land consisting of two acres, bought for 175 dollars from Rebecca Fairchild, was recorded by the Town Clerk. To make the provisions for proper burial complete, the traditional *Hevrah Kaddishah* (Holy Brotherhood), charged with caring for the deceased, was called into existence in the same year. On the other hand, in order to live up to the tradition of providing food and shelter for transient coreligionists who were in need, the *Hachnasat Orehim* (Society for Welcoming Transients) was established at about the same time. With these organizations, the foundations of a Jewish community had been laid.

The life of the early settlers was not an easy one. Trudging with a pack on the back from early morning until late at night, they returned to their lodging houses exhausted and often with little or no earnings. Gathering in one of the houses over a glass of tea they would exchange their daily experiences, gossip, or play games. It was at these gatherings that future plans were discussed regarding themselves, their families and friends, as well as those concerning the budding group life. The difficulties in adjusting themselves to a new and strange environment, the uncertainty and hardship in procuring a livelihood, absorbed most of their attention, so that they took hardly any part in the social and cultural life of the town. Whatever time could be spared from their personal problems was devoted to the affairs of their own group. A favorite pastime of that period, indulged in on Sundays, was visiting the newly acquired burial grounds in Roxbury. This tract of land was thickly strewn with rocks and boulders. Weather permitting, the little group would start for the cemetery early in the morning in buggies, which some of them possessed, for the purpose of removing from it the scattered rocks. There they would spend the day gathering and splitting the stones and placing them on the boundaries of their property so as to form a fence. It is interesting to note that some of these stones later served as the foundation of the synagogue. A sip from a bottle and a bite of herring and "pumpernickel" bread enlivened the party and added to the good time had by all.

By the early nineties the settlers were an organized body, a congregation with some of the necessary paraphernalia but with no permanent quarters. The attic of an empty house on Cedar Street served as the first meeting place of the congregation. After a while the congregation moved to a boarding house opposite the depot, kept by Joe Blum, one of the few who settled down in Stamford with his family. There the Torah and other religious articles were kept and on Saturdays and holidays a room was cleared for the assembled worshippers to hold their service. In time these quarters became too small to accommodate the ever growing congregation. The "synagogue" was then moved to a larger room in the shop of Simon Rosenberg, a tailor, who was living with his family on Hawthorne Street. After a while even these larger quarters became inadequate, owing to a further increase in the Jewish population. There was also a growing demand for three daily services. Accordingly, a store on Greyrock Place was rented and converted into a House of God. On the High Holy Days, however, when the number of worshippers was augmented by an influx of Jews from the neighboring villages, Miller's "Small Hall" on the corner of Main and Pacific Streets was rented to accommodate the congregation.

Simultaneously with these provisions for self-perpetuation, the group sought to adjust itself to the new environment. Most of the individuals in the group showed an eagerness to learn the English language and to acquire a knowledge of the laws and institutions of the country. One of them, who had lived in England for some time before coming to this country and knew some English, acted as an instructor. Many members of the group later joined evening classes in English and citizenship maintained by the town. Parades and patriotic celebrations found eager participants among them. When they grew in numbers, they arranged for such celebrations as a group.

As the century drew to a close, most of the Stamford Jews were still engaged in peddling, but quite a few either owned or were employed in stores, particularly clothing and shoe shops, and some, as we have already noted, were tailors and shoemakers. They had thus become a factor in the economic and social life of the town. Their relations with the rest of the community on the whole differed little from those of other immigrants. Like every newly arrived immigrant group, they encountered prejudice here and there. The few surviving pioneers of the Jewish settlement are unanimous in their claim that they met with no antagonism but, on the contrary, were often received with courtesy and respect by those with whom they had dealings. Certain incidents, however, reported by themselves or recorded in the local press, would seem to indicate that they exaggerated the welcome extended to them and that, in their thankfulness at being allowed to earn their living unmolested, they overlooked a great deal.

Living and working in proximity to the Irish neighborhood they were frequently victims of attacks by the youths of that section, who would throw stones at them and otherwise annoy them. So serious did these annoyances become that on several occasions they were forced to have organized skirmishes with them. Even the pulpit was not entirely free of prejudice. In a sermon preached by a Congregationalist minister and reported in the September 12, 1892 issue of the *Stamford Advocate,* the menace of cholera prevalent at that time was linked to the Jewish newcomers in the community. "If," said the minister, "the threatened invasion of Asiatic cholera through a filthy mass of disgusting Russian Jews shall startle our good natured, easy going nation into a realization of the danger and lead to the exclusion of undesirable Europeans, the pestilence will prove a blessing in disguise."

As late as 1900 and even beyond that date, Jews were looked upon as peculiar, and their customs and ceremonies, as far as they were open to general observation, were regarded as quite outlandish, if not downright queer. Reports regarding the observance of their holidays printed at the time in the local press give proof of that. In describing a New Year's service, a reporter in the *Stamford Telegram* of September 25, 1900, writes: "The hall is crowded with Hebrews of all descriptions; all keep their hats on and all joining occasionally in a weird sort of chant. The rabbi standing on a sort of platform reads to them in Hebrew and occasionally leads in the chanting." Covering a similar service on the Day of Atonement he reports on October 3, 1900: "The hall is divided into two parts, one of which is occupied by worshippers and the other by spectators. In the place of worship is a sort of shrine hidden by cloth with an oriental device embroidered on it. Around this are grouped tables covered with tall lighted candles and the men, dressed in some religious garb, keep bowing their heads toward the shrine, at the same time chanting something in the Jewish language. The hall is crowded with Hebrews of all descriptions."

That Jewish customs and practices were also given fanciful meanings and entirely erroneous interpretations is illustrated in the following item on *Yom Kippur* found in the *Stamford Advocate* of September 22, 1903: "On that day it is a custom among Hebrews to give presents. Large Jewish firms generally have increases in the salaries of their employees and promotions take effect from *Yom Kippur."*

With the turn of the century, the Jewish group took on the aspect of a definitely established community. Doubts and uncertainty as to the future ceased, and many began looking upon Stamford as their home. Jewish-owned stores and shops made their appearance first on Pacific and Canal Streets and later in the chief business center on Main Street. A number of the settlers acquired homes of their own and commenced participating actively in the social and economic life of the town. A rabbi had not as yet been engaged, but the *shohet* (ritual slaughterer), or a learned man from among the group itself, satisfactorily filled the functions of the spiritual leader.{22} When a major controversy arose, a rabbi was brought from out of town to settle the dispute. Occasionally a lay preacher or a cantor passing through town was engaged temporarily. On important holidays some of the well-to-do went to New York in order to take part in services conducted in a regular synagogue. An item in the *Stamford Advocate* of September 17, 1898, referring to the celebration of the Hebrew New Year, closes with the following remark: "Many of the local Hebrews held services in a room in Miller's building on Main Street, while the higher class went to New York." Even as late as 1900, items in the local press indicate, a number of the Stamford Jews preferred spending the High Holy Days in the neighboring metropolis.

The group now began to think seriously of erecting a permanent abode for the congregation. Plans were made for acquiring a building lot for a synagogue and an organization, called the "Hebrew Society," was formed in 1900 for the purpose of carrying out those plans and of collecting the necessary funds. To aid it in this task, a "Ladies' Aid Society" and a "Girls' Society" were called into existence. Within a short period a large enough sum was raised to make a down payment on a piece of land on Greyrock Place, bought for $1,000. The Hebrew Society, assisted by its sister organizations, now went about gathering funds for paying off the mortgage. The largest part of the necessary sum was collected in nickels and dimes. "American" ways of fund raising were not, however, by any means neglected. Balls were given with their inevitable souvenir programs, and full use was made of the usual methods for soliciting funds among Jews outside of Stamford. An item in the *Stamford Advocate* of April 16, 1902 discloses that "the Hebrew Society of Stamford held its first annual ball last evening in Town Hall" and that "one of the city officials was present during part of the evening by invitation." The affair, the report continues, was opened with a concert by Professor Campbell's orchestra and was followed by dancing which lasted until morning.

The efforts of the Hebrew Society were so well supported that on October 7, 1903 a gathering took place to celebrate the clearing of the mortgage. At a mass meeting which was followed by a "herring banquet," the mortgage was formally burned and plans were made for erecting the building. On this occasion the community, which now numbered about 100 families, issued an appeal to its own members as well as to Jews living in nearby towns to help support the "building of a house of God, so that the shame of having to wander from house to house and from tent to tent to supplicate before the Lord may be removed from us."

Only a few months intervened between this ceremony and the actual commencement of building the edifice, for on August 7, 1904, the congregation celebrated the laying of the cornerstone. The ceremony, marked by a great deal of pomp, was attended by every member of the Jewish group as well as by prominent out-of-town rabbis, outstanding local civic leaders, and representatives of all religious denominations. Indeed, according to an account in the *Stamford Advocate* of August 8, 1904, it was the mayor of the town who placed the cornerstone in position and the publisher of the local newspaper who gave the chief address, while the minister of the Congregational Church was among the main speakers. It is quite remarkable to note with what rapidity the group attained status in the community as a whole. Only a little more than a decade elapsed between the time when a handful of itinerants, lacking economic and social status and unnoticed by anyone, hesitatingly formed a temporary association and the day when they became an organized body prominent enough to win the attention of the community and praise from its leaders.

The foundation had been laid, but it took almost four years to complete the building. If the whole structure of the new synagogue could not be finished soon, the basement could. Within a month or so the congregation was housed in the "cellar," as the members called it, proud of having finally a place of their own where they could worship in privacy and hold their gatherings undisturbed.[3]

For years to come, the building of the synagogue demanded most of the attention of the group, but there were other problems of great importance to the growing community, to which time and energy were devoted. Among Jews everywhere, a school for the training of the young in Jewish religion and lore occupies a position second only to a place of worship. Simultaneously, therefore, with the establishment of such a place provisions were made for the systematic instruction of the children. For several years the few children in the community had been instructed in their own homes by one or two volunteers from among the more educated members of the group. As soon as a room for holding services was rented, it was also put to use as a classroom. Thus, in 1902, the store on Greyrock Place used as a place of worship was equipped with benches, and for several hours a day was turned into a schoolroom. A teacher was brought in to instruct the children. At first the "school" was an exact replica of the traditional heder, the acquisition of some skill in reading the Hebrew prayerbook, without understanding the meaning of words, a certain knowledge of the Old Testament in its original, and an acquaintance with religious beliefs and customs being the objectives. With the spread, however, of nationalist or Zionist ideology among the members of the group, attempts were made to modernize the curriculum somewhat and to include the teaching of modern Hebrew as well as Jewish history. Children attended the *Talmud Torah* (institution for the teaching of the Law), as the school was now called, every day of the week, excepting Fridays and Saturdays, after public school hours. The whole community contributing toward its upkeep, the school was open free of charge to all children.

At the beginning of the century, Zionism began to crystallize into a definite political movement, and its ideology and doctrines started to sweep the Jewish masses everywhere. Some of the pioneers of the Jewish settlement in Stamford brought the dream of a revived Zion with them, while others came under the influence of the movement after coming to America. Several members of the group, imbued with the spirit of Jewish nationalism, began seeking a way of spreading the idea of a Jewish homeland as well as means of helping in a concrete manner to build the future Jewish state. Consequently, an organization known as *"L'Maan Zion"* (On Behalf of Zion) was founded in 1902, with the aim of giving moral as well as financial support to the creation of a Jewish state in Palestine. Under the leadership of two ardent Zionists from among the group, the organization began functioning as an agency for raising funds for the upbuilding of Palestine and for disseminating Zionism. Money, in very small amounts, to be sure, was collected for buying colonial shares, planting trees in Palestine, and a variety of other Zionist endeavors.

Frequent meetings were called at which discussions were held and lectures given, all aiming to arouse the interest of the group in Zionism and to get material aid. Spreading the gospel of Zionism was the primary but not by any means the only aim of the society. *"L'Maan Zion"* was chiefly responsible for organizing the aforementioned Talmud Torah, and particularly for injecting into the infant institution a spirit of Jewish nationalism. Immediately after the Kishinef pogrom in 1903, the society sponsored a protest meeting and led a successful drive for funds for the relief of the victims. So active did this small but energetic fraternity become in all affairs of the group that it soon held the undisputed leadership in the tiny community.

Simultaneously with the provisions made for filling its spiritual needs, the group began giving thought to the desirability of organizing for mutual financial aid. Thus, in 1903, a branch of the national Order of Free Sons of Judah was duly organized. To the sick and death benefits paid by the Order, the local lodge added other voluntary aid to members in distress. The year 1903 marks the end of the formative period of the Stamford Jewish community, in which foundations of organized life were laid. The period that follows witnesses the evolution of an obscure group of families, crudely organized for purposes of cultural survival, into a well established community whose importance in the economic and social life of the city was increasingly recognized.

Footnotes
1. The trolley fare from New York to Stamford was 28 cents and the boat fare 25 cents.
2. Undoubtedly a misspelling of Agudath Sholem (Society of Peace).
3. Miller's and St. Joseph's halls, where services were held prior to this time, were located in the heart of the business section. Since the worshippers were plainly visible to anyone passing, crowds would gather to watch their "funny" behavior and willingly or unwillingly annoy them.

CHAPTER VI

REARING THE STRUCTURE

The Russian pogroms of 1903-04 sent forth a renewed wave of immigrants across the Atlantic, the ripples of which soon reached Stamford. The newcomers of this period, at least a goodly number of them, differed somewhat from their predecessors. Although still adherents of the religion of their fathers, they had, as a rule, taken a greater interest in the political and social movements agitating the Jews and the world at large. Zionism as a political doctrine had taken on a more concrete form by that time, and many of the immigrants were so deeply imbued with its philosophy that working for its cause overshadowed all of their other interests. On the other hand, revolutionary socialism, which claimed even larger number of adherents, had a particular fascination for the persecuted Russian Jew, so that he readily joined in the movement for social and economic liberation, and became as ardent a radical and "citizen of the world" as his brother became a Jewish nationalist or Zionist. This was also the time when the Jewish socialists in Russia had organized their own party known as the "Bund," which aimed at spreading the doctrine of socialism among the Jews in the Yiddish language and at the secularization of the Jewish culture. The activities of the Bund served to stimulate the development of Yiddish and a modern Yiddish literature, just as the spread of Zionism aided greatly in advancing the renascence of the Hebrew language and literature.

The new immigrants thus included both ardent Zionists and socialists. While the Zionists, as soon as possible after their arrival in Stamford, joined the little nationalist group, adding strength to its efforts at propagating the ideals of Zionism, the radicals organized a group of their own, with the aim of counteracting them and of disseminating the teachings of socialism. The Zionists considered Hebrew, the symbol of national revival, as the language which was eventually to become the mother tongue of the Jewish nation, although not a few favored the survival of Yiddish alongside Hebrew, the "real" language of the Jews. The socialists, on the other hand, looked upon modern Hebrew as the creation of the nationalistic "bourgeoisie," and regarded Yiddish as the language of the people. Aloof from these two contending elements stood the orthodox Jew intent upon continuing his old-time religion with as little modification as possible, and adhering to Yiddish as the language of everyday life and to Hebrew as the holy tongue of the Bible and prayerbook. He looked with disdain upon the attempts to give new political and ideological meanings to either Yiddish or Hebrew.

Owing to the influx of new blood, the Jewish community entered upon a period of rapid expansion as well as of differentiation. The former community of interests began to be displaced by a diversity of aims. Not all were orthodox anymore; not all were Zionists; not all were peddlers and shopkeepers.[1] The organizations and institutions founded previously received new members, to be sure, making it possible for them to expand; but new, "strange" organizations, not entirely to the liking of the "old" pioneers, sprang up and took their place in Jewish communal life, lending a more diversified character to the community.

As intimated above, the groups of immigrants who began to arrive in 1904-05 included individuals differing in their economic, social and political outlooks. Some, to be sure, fitted right into the existing organizations and institutions and, hence, lent their hand in building them up, but others preferred, and were sometimes even forced, to organize according to their own ideas. Thus, although there already existed a mutual benefit society — a branch of the Order of Free Sons of Judah, a group of newcomers, owing partly to their not being acceptable to the members of the existing lodge because of their economic status, were forced, in 1905, to form their own society under the name of Workers' Benevolent Association.{23} This name may be somewhat misleading, as the people organizing the society were far from being class-conscious workers. They were just poverty-stricken, struggling immigrants, usually engaged in the type of work which their predecessors, now economically better situated, had been or still were engaged in. Being ardently pious and subscribing to Hassidic doctrines, they were also the cause of a rift in the so far smoothly functioning religious life of the community. Since they insisted upon following their own form of worship, namely, the Sephardic, which differed somewhat from that of the established congregation, the Ashkenazic, they were excluded from the latter, and were forced to organize into a separate congregation which conducted its services in the basement of a private home instead of the "cellar" of the regular synagogue. This was the first open rift in the organized life of the community, but it was of short duration and no consequence. No fundamental issues being involved, as soon as they had become "acclimated" and achieved status, the members of the dissenting group applied and were admitted into the national Order of the Western Star, as the Julia Herzl Lodge, and to the congregation as members of good standing.[2]

Much more indicative of the cleavages occurring in the life of the community was the establishment of a branch of the national Workmen's Circle in the same year, 1905. Although primarily a benefit society, the Circle was an organization composed of Jewish workers and artisans, aiming at making the Jewish workingmen class-conscious and at spreading among them the gospel of socialism. All Jewish socialists and bundists, 25 in number, joined the branch and promptly declared ideological warfare on the Zionists and the rest of the "bourgeois" community with its "capitalist" practices.

Partly to counteract the activities of the radicals, an additional Zionist society, the "Zion Camp" was called into existence in 1907. The primary aim of this organization was work and propaganda for the Zionist cause. As an additional inducement to prospective members to join as well as to those who had already joined, to remain in the organization, the society offered sick and death benefits, and later became a branch of the fraternal Order of Sons of Zion. With two organizations and a much larger membership, and with the weight of Jewish public opinion on their side, the Zionists could now successfully undertake a battle of words with the radicals who, strangely enough, they thought, refused to learn a plain lesson of history— that the Jewish problem can be solved only by a return of the Jew to his ancient home in Palestine.

For almost four years the basement of the proposed synagogue building had to serve the congregation as a home. On the High Holy Days, when the "cellar" could not accommodate all the worshippers, Miller's or St. Joseph's Hall still had to be used. But in 1905, with about 125 families, the congregation felt numer-

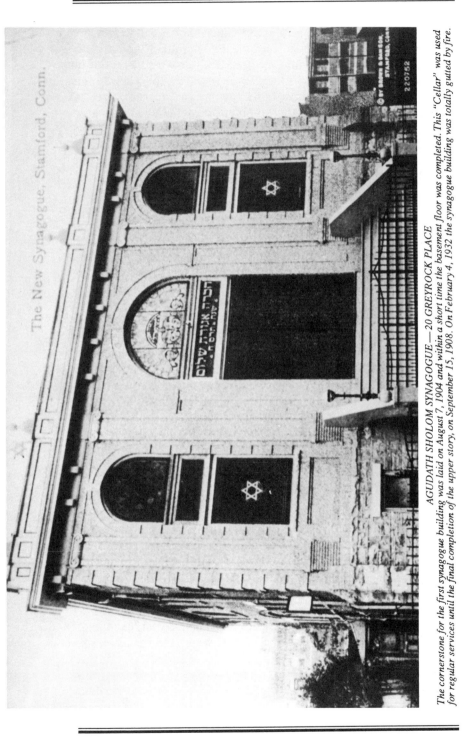

The New Synagogue, Stamford, Conn.

AGUDATH SHOLOM SYNAGOGUE — 20 GREYROCK PLACE
The cornerstone for the first synagogue building was laid on August 7, 1904 and within a short time the basement floor was completed. This "Cellar" was used for regular services until the final completion of the upper story, on September 15, 1908. On February 4, 1932 the synagogue building was totally gutted by fire.

ous and prosperous enough to have its own shohet and to support its own butcher. Donations toward the completion of the building were meanwhile flowing into the treasury in a small but steady stream. In 1907, an entry in the *pinkas* (record book kept by the synagogue), states that a board of directors was formed to act as a building committee for the completion of the synagogue. A constitution of the congregation was also written and published in Yiddish in the same year. Paragraph 2 of this document sets forth that "all transactions as well as all records of the congregation shall be in the Yiddish-German language." The following paragraph sets forth that "the aim of the congregation shall be, first, to maintain a meeting house, a place for daily, evening and morning prayers, and second, that the services conducted shall from now on and forever be in the orthodox (Ashkenazic) manner."

The plans of the building, as given in the *Stamford Advocate* of March 21, 1904, call for a structure having "a front of 25 feet 8 inches and a depth of 67 feet. The design...suggests a Hebrew style of architecture...The main entrance is from the porch with broad steps and paneled hand railing...The auditorium is trimmed with oak finished in a dark shade, while pulpit, desk, pews, gallery seats and furniture are also in oak." Since the synagogue was also to provide for the educational needs of the community, the basement of the building was to serve as schoolrooms. On the other hand, to fill the need for the ritual bath, a practice to which many of the group still adhered, a plunge pool *(mikvah),* was to be erected in the rear of the building. "This," the news item continues, "will be built of brick with galvanized cornice and slate roof. The receptacle or tank is to be lined with white tiles and have a floor of cement."

Although these plans were made in 1904, it was not until the spring of 1908 that actual work on the building started. On September 15 of that year the synagogue was finished — in time for the congregation to celebrate the High Holy Days in its own home. An entry in the *pinkas* lists 60 pew holders who paid for their pews the sum of $7,915, the highest price for a pew being $175 and the lowest $50. The synagogue started with about one hundred members, each of whom paid $12 a year in dues. For this a member was entitled to a seat for the entire year, except on the High Holy days when special tickets were sold for all seats. Other benefits accruing to the member included free burial ground, $35 paid to his family to defray funeral expenses, and provision for *kaddish* (prayer for the deceased) in case he died without male issue.[3] No regular rabbi was engaged for many years to come.{24} The yearly budget of the synagogue was between $3,500 and $4,000 and was covered by membership dues, occasional donations, and the sale of seats for *Rosh Hashanah* and *Yom Kippur*. This did not include payments on the mortgage which were met entirely by voluntary gifts. The lots adjoining the synagogue on both sides were soon acquired in order to prevent building in the immediate vicinity, and with the planting of a lawn and trees around it, the building took its place among the other houses of worship in Stamford.

As the synagogue increased in membership and wealth, its importance in the Jewish community grew. Aside from providing for purely religious needs, it housed and controlled the daily Hebrew school, maintained the *Hevrah Kaddishah* (Holy Burial Society), and supervised the distribution of kosher meat. All communal affairs were held in its building, and all "respectable" Jews belonged to it directly or indirectly. This central position of the synagogue in the life of the community was, however, quite short-lived, and, as will be brought out later, its significance was largely lost in subsequent years.

By 1908 a number of individuals in the community thought it desirable to form another lodge which would be more selective, and hence more fitting for them, as businessmen, to belong to. The result was the formation in that year of a branch of the Independent Order of Brith Abraham, a national fraternal order, under the name of Fairfield County Lodge. Soon, however, a still more exclusive organization appeared, which began to rival the new lodge, despite the fact that it offered no financial benefits in return for dues paid. This was a branch of the B'nai B'rith whose primary aim was to fight anti-Semitism as it made its appearance in the business and professional world. The founding in 1910 of the Jacob Ullman Lodge, as the branch was called, did not affect the membership rolls of the other lodges, for it did not compete with them; but the lodge did attract the more prosperous or aspiring business and professional men, since membership soon came to be considered a mark of social superiority. The year 1910 marked also the founding of three other communal organizations. The desire of some immigrants to organize according to country of birth found its realization in the establishment of the Austro-Hungarian Benevolent Association, which, in addition to offering sick and death benefits to its members, aimed at bringing together individuals hailing from the former provinces of the Austro-Hungarian empire for the purpose of strengthening their common ties. The need for free loans felt by peddlers and small shopkeepers was met by the establishment of a *Gemilat Hesed* (Free Loan Society). The third organization formed that year was the Ladies' Educational League for the purpose of aiding in the support of the Hebrew school.

Soon after the completion of the synagogue building, in 1909, the school, till then located in a store on Greyrock Place, was moved to the basement of the building and renamed *Beth-Sefer Zioni* (Zionist school) — indicating that it was under the control of the Zionists. Although most parents saw nothing wrong in sending their children every day after school hours to Hebrew school, some even claiming that two hours a day were inadequate, there were already a large number of Americanized individuals who condemned such a practice, claiming that it was too much of a burden on the child, and that instruction given once a week, preferably on a Sunday, would be sufficient for the child to acquire a knowledge of the essentials of Judaism. With the coming into existence, in 1911, of a branch of the Council of Jewish Women, a national charitable organization of wives of middle-class business men and professionals, those holding the latter view had their way. They organized a Sunday school alongside the existing Hebrew school, teaching the principles of Judaism in the English language and attracting the children of the wealthier and more Americanized class. The previous agreement as to what type of education Jewish children in the community should receive thus came to an end.

The emergence of a left wing in the Zionist movement, the so-called Poale Zionists, had its repercussions in the Stamford Jewish community. In 1915, a branch of the Jewish National Workers' Alliance, a fraternal order aiming at a synthesis of Zionism and socialism, was organized by the more radically inclined Zionists and right-wing socialists from the Workmen's Circle, bringing disagreement also into the Zionist camp.

The increased prosperity which the first years of the World War brought to members of the Jewish community, the renewed hopes of a brighter day for Jewry, and, above all, the growing self-assurance that comes with a more settled mode of life, resulted in greater activity among the members of the community on behalf of various Jewish communal and national causes. Zionism seemed nearer realization than ever before, and, as a result, the Zionists became the most dynamic force in the community,

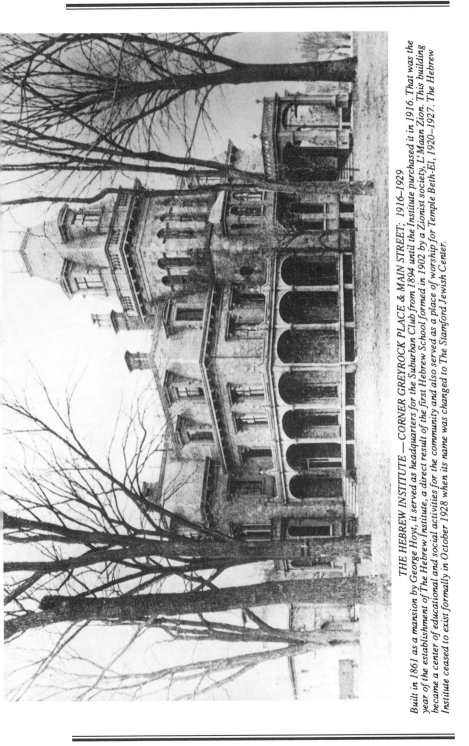

THE HEBREW INSTITUTE — CORNER GREYROCK PLACE & MAIN STREET; 1916–1929

Built in 1861 as a mansion by George Hoyt, it served as headquarters for the Suburban Club from 1894 until the Institute purchased it in 1916. That was the year of the establishment of The Hebrew Institute, a direct result of the first Hebrew School formed in 1902 by a Zionist society, L'Maan Zion. This building became a center of educational and social activities for the community and also served as a place of worship for Temple Beth-El, 1920–1927. The Hebrew Institute ceased to exist formally in October 1928 when its name was changed to The Stamford Jewish Center.

assuming unquestioned leadership in Jewish communal affairs. It was owing to them that in 1916 a building on Greyrock Place was bought and renovated, at a cost of approximately $15,000, to house the Hebrew school and provide room for the growing activities of the community. The Zionists also sponsored a number of youth organizations for the purpose of inculcating in the children and youth the ideals of Zionism as well as of aiding in the cause. Branches of the national youth organization, Young Judea, were organized as the Palestine Seniors, consisting of children between the ages of 16-18; the Palestine Juniors, admitting boys between 11-14; the Deborah Club for girls of 11-14; and the Blossom Club, comprising girls of 15-17. A Hebrew Club, consisting of graduates of the Hebrew school and aiming at extending their acquired education and Jewish interests, and the Louis D. Brandeis Zion Society, a Zionist organization for American-born or Americanized young men, were other results of these efforts. All activities now took place in the Hebrew Institute, as the building was called, with the Zionists as the moving spirit. To further strengthen their cause, they organized in 1918 an officially sanctioned local, the so-called District of the Zionist Organization of America, which cooperated closely with other Zionist societies.

The left and right wings of Zionism, namely, the Poale Zionists, who clung to Yiddish, and the recently organized Mizrahists, who clung tenaciously to orthodox religion, were also awakened to renewed activity. In 1917, a young immigrant from Russia organized a branch of the Poale Zion and introduced cultural and Zionist-Socialist activities in the Yiddish language. He arranged for lectures and debates, and organized reading circles and courses in Yiddish literature. Although showing little activity, the Zionistically inclined orthodox Jews nevertheless managed to form an organization of their own, a branch of the *Mizrahi,* a world-wide organization of religious Zionists, with the aim of propagating the idea of a religious Zionism and of aiding their party.

With the entry of the United States into the World War, the main interests of the members of the community were absorbed by the more vital problems of the day, leaving little room for Zionist and other cultural activities. Some of the active members either enlisted in the American army or joined the Jewish Legion, organized by England for service in Palestine. In 1917, however, the community was spurred on to new efforts by the declaration of the British Government, known as the Balfour Declaration, proclaiming the restoration of Palestine as a Jewish national

TEMPLE BETH-EL — 144 PROSPECT STREET 1927–1973
Built 1927 and used for regular worship services prior to its final completion and dedication in 1928. Designed in the classical revival style of Greco-Roman

homeland, and by the plight of the Eastern European Jews. Money-raising campaigns were carried on successfully, netting large sums for the Palestine restoration funds as well as for the relief of distressed Jewish communities in Eastern Europe. At this time efforts were concentrated on the material needs of Zionism and on relief work, and emphasis upon the cultural phase was considerably lessened.

The years immediately following the war found the Jewish community in Stamford rapidly reaching the age of maturity. Most of the members of the community were still clinging to the cultural heritage they brought with them. Many, however, were well on the way to become Americanized, while a goodly number were in the process of completely identifying themselves with the American scene, or at least trying to do so. If to these are added the growing number of American-born young people — children of the early settlers — and the Americanized Jews who settled in Stamford in those years, it can readily be seen that the community was in the process of becoming divided into two major groups — those trying to transplant and perpetuate the Jewish cultural patterns prevalent in Eastern Europe with as little change as possible, and those willing to make extensive concessions to the American environment.

The ideological rift that had resulted in the organizing of the Sunday school by the Council of Jewish Women some years prior to the war now became much more pronounced. An ever growing number of people of influence in the community considered the type of services conducted in the synagogue unsatisfactory and ill adapted to the needs of Americanized Jews. By 1920 they mustered enough strength to organize a congregation that would meet their requirements. The new congregation was of the so-called "conservative" type, which introduced extensive reforms in the old ritual and permitted departure from orthodox religious observances. Not feeling strong enough to build its own place of worship, the congregation, which assumed the name of Temple Beth-El, met for prayer, not without a previous struggle, in the auditorium of the Hebrew Institute. Soon the Sunday school conducted by the Council of Jewish Women merged with the weekly religious school started by the new congregation, adding another inducement for joining the Temple. In 1921, the congregation grew large enough to engage its own rabbi. With a spiritual leader of its own the congregation embarked upon intensive activities. In 1922 the women members formed the Beth-El Sisterhood,

CORNERSTONE LAYING FOR THE JEWISH COMMUNITY CENTER, 132 PROSPECT STREET
Left to Right: Jacob Weissman, Manuel Chausky, Hyman Frankel; November 25, 1928.

while the children were organized into the Junior Beth-El. In 1925 the congregation purchased its own cemetery, and in the following year it engaged a permanent cantor.

The Jewish community at this time was enjoying the general prosperity of the mid-twenties, and readily embarked upon an ambitious building program. Besides plans for a separate house of worship for members of Beth-El, plans were made for moving the Hebrew Institute to new quarters to meet the increased needs of the community. The building of a Community Center was, in fact, proposed by members of the Institute. The directors of the Hebrew Institute tried to dissuade the Beth-El group from proceeding with their plans for a separate building, arguing that it would be too much of a burden upon the community to build and maintain two expensive plants, and suggesting that the congregation be housed in the proposed center. But the members of the budding congregation were determined to go ahead with their plans, believing that only by having a home of their own would they be able to worship God and conduct their affairs in their own manner.

Both sides being set in their intentions, they proceeded simultaneously to plan the erection of two buildings. The Temple, completed in September 1927, was the first to be finished. Built at a cost of approximately $125,000 in one of the better sections of the town, so-called Strawberry Hill Section, the edifice is thus described in its Dedication Book:

> The building has been designed in the Greek Classic Style. It has a large central entrance portico with an imposing colonnade of stone Ionic Columns. The portico leads to the memorial foyer which runs the entire depth of the building, leading to the Synagogue in the front and to the Social Hall in the rear. The Synagogue which will seat 200 persons comfortably immediately adjoins the Social Hall which will seat about 300 persons. These two rooms are connected by means of folding doors which, when open, will make one large assembly room on the first floor seating about 500 persons.

> The Classic Style has been modified to a Colonial treatment for the interior of the Synagogue and the Social Hall. These rooms have a vaulted ceiling. The wall treatment has pilaster and large circular head windows in which memorial windows will be placed. The Rabbi's room and Choir Loft immediately adjoining the pulpits are at the front of the building. The Social Hall and large stage and dressing rooms in connection with it are at the rear of the building. The kitchen,

THE STAMFORD JEWISH CENTER — 132 PROSPECT STREET

The new JCC in 1930 offered health and physical education facilities, with a gymnasium and swimming pool. Also included was a bowling alley, billiard room, auditorium, dining room, classrooms for the Hebrew School, and a day camp serving pantry and ladies' retiring rooms and rest rooms are also provided on this main floor. A commodious stair leads from the memorial foyer on the first floor to the school rooms on the floor below. On this floor, which is entirely above the ground and which has a clear height of 11'0", are an assembly hall, six class rooms, a library, executive office, men's rooms and coat rooms. This school room floor may also be reached by its own entrance on the school side of the building; this entrance permits the use of this floor without using the main entrance of the building. The class rooms which accommodate about 25 children each are well ventilated with large windows.

The building is built of light color grey brick with stone columns and pediment. The floors are of oak and all walls and ceilings are plastered with sand-finish plaster.

The Community Center, completed and formally dedicated about two years later, on January 19, 1930, was erected on a site only a few yards away from the Temple. Costing well over $200,000, it is an extensive, substantially built four-story brick structure, containing on the lower floor a well equipped gymnasium, shower rooms, pool, health room, bowling alleys, billiard room and other facilities; on the ground floor a roomy, well appointed lobby, an auditorium seating 550, stage and dressing rooms, offices, library room, social room, and rest rooms; and on the upper floor class and club rooms. Thus, although the sale of the Institute building brought in about $60,000, the raising of the new structure meant an additional expenditure by the community of much more than twice the amount.

The erection of a new synagogue building necessitated by the burning down of the old one on February 4, 1932, completed the transformation of the physical plant of the Jewish community. The new synagogue was built on Grove Street in one of the better residential sections near the business center. Completed, except for interior details, in September 1938, the building, a handsome brick structure, accommodates 1,000 worshippers, and contains in the basement a large hall, vestry, kitchen and rest rooms. When entirely finished the building will have cost $90,000. Part of the building in the rear constitutes the ritual pool *(mikvah)*, built in a modern design and in accordance with the latest sanitary requirements.

The post-war years brought with them a further division of interests and ramification of activities. The spread of a religious reform movement with its "strange" doctrines was viewed with suspicion by the orthodox as well as by many of the Zionist and

AGUDATH SHOLOM SYNAGOGUE — 29 GROVE STREET: 1938–1965

On July 29, 1934 the ground floor of the new synagogue was dedicated but it was not until 1938 that the first High Holiday Services were held in the nearly completed upper structure.

radical elements of the community. Partly because of a reaction to that movement, but largely owing to new trends in the cultural life of Jewry, each of these groups initiated new activities and founded new agencies to further its own causes. The orthodox element organized in 1921 the *Vaad Hair* (City Council), a traditional institution prevalent in Jewish communities of Eastern Europe, to effect a stricter supervision over religious affairs, particularly those pertaining to *kashrut* (kosher meat) in the community. They engaged a rabbi of their own. They also tried, with considerable success, to impose their religious views upon the otherwise mainly nationalistic Hebrew school. The Zionists, too, made an effort to intensify their work by putting new life into their "District," by organizing in 1924 a branch of the Hadassah, the women's Zionist organization, and by injecting more Zionism into the Hebrew school curriculum. The radicals, organized in the Workmen's Circle, on the other hand, opened their own school and began to intensify their cultural activities. The opening of an elementary school with Yiddish as the language of instruction and main subject occurred soon after the split of the Workmen's Circle into left and right wings in 1925. It was the leftist group in the organization that established the school in a building on Pacific Street. For a while the rightists consented to send their children to the school operated by their left-wing colleagues in preference to sending them to the existing Hebrew school. But in 1929, when the leftists seceded from the Circle and shortly afterwards affiliated themselves with the newly established, communistically-inclined International Workers' Order, the right-wingers organized a Yiddish school of their own, bringing up to four the number of schools functioning in the Jewish community at the time.

A goodly number of the more Amercanized members of the community now regarded belonging to strictly Jewish organizations as altogether insufficient. Joining non-Jewish or non-sectarian societies began to be looked upon as highly desirable as well as advantageous. As a result Jews now joined every non-Jewish organization open to them to the extent of converting at least one of them, the Excelsior Lodge #49 of the Knights of Pythias, into a largely Jewish branch. Not being welcomed into the two existing Masonic Lodges, the Jews founded, in 1922, a lodge of their own the Roosevelt Lodge.

We come thus to the end of tracing the evolution of a tiny group of bewildered individuals into a good-sized, well estab-

SANCTUARY OF AGUDATH SHOLOM SYNAGOGUE — 29 GROVE STREET 1938–1965
Conforming with Orthodox tradition, the women's sections on both sides of the sanctuary were elevated, serving as a mechitza or separation in seating from the men.

lished community. In the preceding pages an attempt was made to present a picture of the community in the making; in the pages that follow attention will be concentrated upon a portrayal of the functioning of that community and its adjustments to the life surrounding it.

Footnotes

1. In 1905, according to the testimony of several old Jewish residents, approximately 200 Jewish workers found employment in the Yale and Towne factory and a Canadian automobile factory operating at that time in town.
2. Since this was the name of Theodor Herzl, head of the world Zionist movement, it is apparent that the members were Zionists.
3. *Kaddish* is a prayer that, according to orthodox belief, must be said thrice daily by the sons of the deceased for a year after his death.

CHAPTER VII

THE ECONOMIC PICTURE [1]

The Stamford Jewish community comprises 3,279 individuals, constituting about five per cent of the total population of the town. As shown on Table 1 and Chart I, over two thirds of the Stamford Jews are native born. Almost half of the natives were born in Stamford, and close to one third of them are of either native or mixed parentage. Of those born abroad, about two thirds come from Russia and most of the rest from Poland and former Austria-Hungary, particularly Galicia. Rumania has contributed 45 persons and Germany only 9. A division by sex shows 1,610 males and 1,546 females. As brought out in Chart II, the most numerous age group is the one between 21 and 44 which includes 1,475 persons. The next largest groups are those of 45 to 59 and 5 to 13, with 475 and 428 respectively. As is further shown in Table I, the number of individuals under 21 who were born abroad is entirely negligible, owing to the fact that there have been few immigrants in recent years. Even this number would be considerably smaller were it not for a small number of Austrian refugees who have recently settled in town.

The community consists of a total of 960 families, ranging from one to ten members each. Of these, 528, or 55 per cent, are "foreign," and 396, or 41.2 per cent are "native," the nativity of 36 being unknown.[2] The most common type of family, as can be gleaned from Table 2, is the four-person family, of which there are 259. Next in order of their numerical importance are the three-person family with a total of 211, the two-person with 198, the five-person with 119, the one-person with 72, and the six-person with only 45. Of the remaining types none is of numerical significance. Comparing the "foreign" with the "native" families,

TABLE 1
DISTRIBUTION OF STAMFORD JEWS ACCORDING TO NATIVITY, BY SEX AND AGE, 1938

Age and Sex	All Groups		Native				Foreign Born							Unknown
	Number	Per Cent	Total:	Foreign Parentage	Mixed Parentage	Native Parentage	Total:	Russia	Poland	Austria Hungary	Rumania	Germany	Other	
Total Population	3,279		2,178*	1,506	268	404	978	642	102	131	45	9	49	123
Per Cent		100.0	66.4	45.9	8.2	12.3	29.8	19.5	3.1	4.0	1.4	0.3	1.5	3.8
Male	1,610	49.1	1,093	745	141	207	517	348	53	66	25	3	22	
Female	1,546	47.1	1.085	761	127	197	461	294	49	65	20	6	27	
Unknown	123	3.8												
Under 1 year	37	1.1	37	3	7	27								
Male	18		18	2	4	12								
Female	19		19	1	3	15								
1-4 years	150	4.6	148	18	52	78	2			1			1	
Male	71		71	7	29	35								
Female	79		77	11	23	43	2			1			1	
5-13 years	428	13.1	426	146	111	169	2						2	
Male	217		216	73	52	91	1						1	
Female	211		210	73	59	78	1						1	
14-17 years	210	6.4	208	114	43	51	2		1				1	
Male	105		104	55	23	26	1		1					
Female	105		104	59	20	25	1						1	
18-20 years	176	5.4	175	127	23	25	1			1				
Male	97		96	70	13	13	1			1				
Female	79		79	57	10	12								
21-44 years	1,475	45.0	1,071	992	31	48	404	240	54	56	15	5	34	
Male	734		527	481	19	27	207	127	29	28	7	1	15	
Female	741		544	511	12	21	197	113	25	28	8	4	19	
45-59 years	475	14.5	96	90	1	5	379	267	33	47	24	2	6	
Male	262		55	51	1	3	207	146	15	27	14	1	4	
Female	213		41	39		2	172	121	18	20	10	1	2	
60 years & older	205	6.3	17	16		1	188	135	14	26	6	2	5	
Male	106		6	6			100	75	8	10	4	1	2	
Female	99		11	10		1	88	60	6	16	2	1	3	
Age Unknown	123	3.8												

*Of these 1,005, or 30.7%, were born in Stamford.

we note little difference in size until we reach the more numerous ones, namely, those of five or more. As Table 2 discloses, there are proportionately many fewer large families among the "native" than among the "foreign" families. This is especially true of the six- and seven-person families. No native family comprises more than seven members. Finally, the medium size of the Jewish family is 3.41 which is somewhat lower than the 3.54 given by the United States Census for Stamford as a whole.

According to data obtained in 1938 from 924 of the total of 960 families, only 21 households show that none of their members is gainfully employed. Of these, as seen in Table 3, twenty

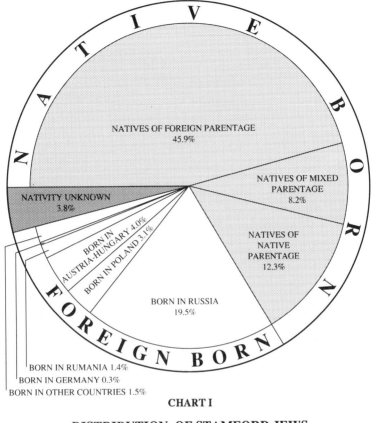

CHART I

DISTRIBUTION OF STAMFORD JEWS
ACCORDING TO NATIVITY
1938

belong to the "foreign" and one to the "native" families. Consulting again Table 3, we note that in the great majority of homes only one person is the provider. In over one fourth of the households two persons share the burden of maintenance. In 91 families there are three, and in only 48 are four or more people gainfully employed. Comparing again the "foreign" with the "native" families, we find that the latter, as can be seen in the same Table, tend to be more of the one-provider and much less of the two-provider type than the former. Again, while among the "foreign" families there are quite a number in which three and four or more persons work for the upkeep of the home, among the "natives" there are very few such families.

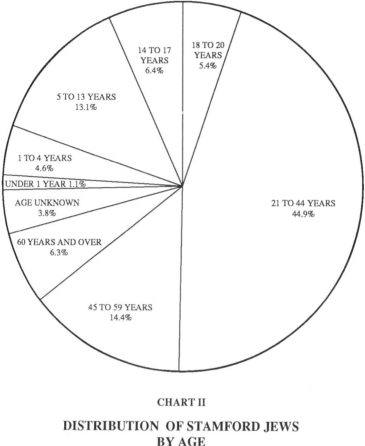

CHART II

DISTRIBUTION OF STAMFORD JEWS
BY AGE
1938

Stamford, as we have seen, may be looked upon as belonging to the New York metropolitan area. As such it provides homes for a considerable number of people whose business connections are in New York. Similarly, quite a few New York residents have their businesses, particularly factories in Stamford, and consequently take part in the economic, and, in certain cases, also in the social life of the town. It is among these two categories of people that some of the wealthiest families are found, and it is mainly owing to them that the per capita wealth of Stamford, as expressed in the median value of homes owned and the median monthly rent paid, is higher than that for the State as a whole or for any of the Connecticut towns of similar size. The Jewish community shares these characteristics with the general community. Most of the wealthiest Jewish families belong to either of the two above-mentioned classes. Were these left out of account, as they properly should be, since the great majority of them do not identify themselves with the Jewish community, the economic class structure of the community would show few extremes.

TABLE 2
DISTRIBUTION OF STAMFORD JEWISH FAMILIES ACCORDING TO SIZE, BY NATIVITY OF HEAD, 1938

Number of Persons Comprising Family*	Total				Native			
	Number	P.C.	Foreign Born	Total	Foreign Parentage	Native Parentage	Unknown
All Groups	960		528	396	381	15	36
Per Cent		100.0	55.0	41.3			3.7
1 person	72	7.5	33	39	35	4	
2 persons	197	20.5	93	105	102	3	
3 persons	211	22.0	109	102	97	5	
4 persons	259	27.0	147	112	111	1	
5 persons	120	12.5	88	32	30	2	
6 persons	45	4.7	41	4	4		
7 persons	13	1.4	11	2	2		
8 persons	4	0.4	4				
9 persons	2	0.2	2				
10 persons	1	0.1	1				
Unknown	36	3.7					
Average size	3.42		3.71	3.03	3.05	2.60	
Median size of Jewish family	3.41		3.70	3.03	3.05	2.60	
Median size of Stamford non-Jewish family**	3.54		4.25	3.04			

*The term "family" in this tabulation has the same meaning as in the United States Census of 1930: "A group of persons related either by blood or marriage or adoption, who live together as one household, usually sharing the same table. Single persons living alone are counted as families."

**Taken from the United States Census of 1930.

TABLE 3
DISTRIBUTION OF STAMFORD JEWISH FAMILIES ACCORDING TO NUMBER OF GAINFUL WORKERS, BY NATIVITY OF HEAD, 1938

Nativity		Number of Gainful Workers					
	Total	0	1	2	3	4 or more	Unknown
All Families	960	21	516	248	91	48	36
Foreign Born	528	20	221	160	84	43	
Native	396	1	295	88	7	5	
Unknown	36						
PER CENT							
All Families	100.0	2.2	53.8	25.8	9.5	5.0	3.7
Foreign Born	100.0	3.8	41.9	30.3	15.9	8.1	
Native	100.0	0.3	74.4	22.2	1.8	1.3	

Since no other data were obtainable, figures on the number of families renting and owning homes and on the assessed value of the homes owned had to be resorted to in order to get some idea of the economic status of the Jewish community. An investigation shows that the percentage of families among the Jews owning and renting homes is about the same as for the community at large. Approximately 30 per cent own their homes and 70 per cent rent them, which is about the same as for the community at large. As observable in Table 4, almost twice as many "foreign" as "native" families in the Jewish community own their homes. The largest percentage of homes owned falls in the $10,000-$14,990 class;

TABLE 4

DISTRIBUTION OF STAMFORD JEWISH FAMILIES ACCORDING TO TENURE AND ASSESSED VALUE OF OWNED HOME*, BY NATIVITY OF HEAD, 1938

Nativity	Total		Tenure**						Assessed Value of Owned Home							Median Value in Dollars	Average Value in Dollars
	No.	P.C.	Rented No.	P.C.	Owned No.	P.C.	Unknown No.	P.C.	Under $3,000	$3,000 to $4,999	$5,000 to $7,499	$7,500 to $9,999	$10,000 to $14,999	$15,000 to $19,999	$20,000 and Over		
All Groups	960	100.0	677	70.5	279	29.1	4	0.4	2	13	50	78	97	19	20	9,887	11,582
Foreign	528	100.0	342	64.8	186	35.2			2	12	39	51	63	10	9	9,460	10,132
Native	396	100.0	317	80.1	75	18.9	4	1.0		1	11	23	31	7	2	10,403	11,353
Unknown	36	100.0	18	50.0	18	50.0						4	3	2	9	19,999	27,522

*For ownership of homes the latest editions of the Stamford City Directory and "Real Estate on the Grand List" published by the Town and City of Stamford were consulted. The assessed value of owned home is to be found in the last named publication.

**According to the City Directory of 1939, Stamford has 15,506 homes. Of these about 30% are owned and about 70% rented.

of these there are 97. Most of the rest are in the $7,500-$9,999 class of which there are 78, and in the $5,000-$7,499 category to which 50 belong. Only two homes owned have an assessed value of less than $3,000; 19 are evaluated at $15,000-$19,999; and 20 at $20,000 and over. It is noteworthy that almost half of the homes in the highest class are owned by families who could not be reached because of a complete lack of connection between them and the community, and that the homes of the highest median as well as average value belong to them.

The Jewish population of Stamford includes 2,436 individuals 16 years of age and older, of which 1,252 are males and 1,184 females. Of these, 1,540 are gainfully occupied. Dividing them according to nativity, we note that well over half of the gainful workers are American born. As shown in Table 5, only slightly over one fourth, or 420, of all the gainfully occupied are females. Most of the gainful female workers, as further disclosed by Table 5, are native-born. Indeed, native-born women workers outnumber those of foreign birth almost 3 to 1.

The number of gainfully employed workers between 16 and 17 years of age, as shown in Chart III, is entirely negligible. Youths between the ages of 18-20 make up only 4.2 per cent of the total number of gainful workers. The largest percentage of gainful workers, as noticed in Table 5, are drawn from the 24-34 age class. Individuals between the ages of 35 and 44 make up the next largest percentage of workers, and those between 45 and 50 the next largest. A little over 11 per cent of individuals in the 21-24 age class and only about 5 per cent of those 60 and over are gainful workers.

The main occupation of the Stamford Jews, as brought out in Chart IV, is trade and commerce. Well over half, or 807, of all gainfully occupied individuals are either in business for themselves or connected otherwise with a commercial enterprise. The main concentration is in the retail rather than the wholesale trade. The fields in which Jews predominate are dry goods and wearing apparel, particularly men's clothing and children's wear, food, jewelry, drugs and cosmetics, furniture, and electrical and plumbing supplies. The relative position held by the Jews in these business fields becomes apparent when their number is checked against that of non-Jews. The Stamford City Directory of 1939 has been used for this purpose.

Of the 16 dealers in men's clothing listed in the Directory, 15 are Jews. All of the five children's and infants' wear shops

TABLE 5
OCCUPATIONAL DISTRIBUTION OF GAINFUL WORKERS 16 YEARS OF AGE AND OVER, BY AGE, SEX AND NATIVITY, FOR STAMFORD JEWS, 1938

Occupation	All Groups Total	All Groups M	All Groups F	Native Total	Native M	Native F	Foreign Born Total	Foreign Born M	Foreign Born F	Nativity and Age Unknown	16-17	18-20	21-24	25-34	35-44	45-59	60 & over
Total Population 16 Years and Over	2,436																
Gainfully Occupied	1,540	1,120	420	859	577	282	575	468	107	106	6	65	179	422	368	306	88
Per Cent	100.0	72.7	27.3	55.8	37.5	18.3	37.3	30.4	6.9	6.9	0.4	4.2	11.6	27.4	23.9	19.9	5.7
Trade and Commerce	807	608	199	454	332	122	353	276	77		5	35	72	231	212	192	60
Automobiles and accessories	23	22	1	17	16	1	6	6				2	2	9	8	1	1
Banks and finance	17	14	3	12	9	3	5	5						5	7	5	
Beverages and liquor	49	39	10	24	20	4	25	19	6			2	4	25	13	5	
Builders supplies	65	53	12	40	31	9	25	22	3		1	7	11	20	11	11	4
Cigars and stationery stores	45	31	14	16	12	4	29	19	10			1	2	13	16	11	2
Department stores	22	9	13	19	8	11	3	1	2				1	1	5	13	2
Drugs and cosmetics	31	23	8	21	15	6	10	8	2				3	11	13	3	1
Dry goods and wearing apparel	198	118	80	108	64	44	90	54	36			6	17	55	53	42	25
Food stores and dealers	152	124	28	74	59	15	78	65	13		3	13	16	32	35	44	9
Furniture	32	27	5	20	16	4	12	11	1				6	10	5	8	3
Gasoline stations	18	16	2	13	11	2	5	5					1	11	4	2	
Hucksters and peddlers	15	14	1	1	1		14	13	1				1	1	5	8	
Insurance and real estate	39	37	2	26	24	2	13	13						12	9	13	5
Jewelry	27	15	12	17	7	10	10	5	5		1	2	3	4	6	9	2
Miscellaneous	74	66	8	46	39	7	28	27	1			2	5	22	21	18	6
Industry	231	176	55	122	78	44	109	98	11		1	15	43	43	58	57	14
Building	56	51	5	21	16	5	35	35				1	4	7	19	21	4
Clothing	39	27	12	13	7	6	26	20	6				3	4	14	14	4
Food	24	20	4	12	10	2	12	10	2				4	5	9	4	2
Iron, steel and other metals	36	29	7	18	11	7	18	18				2	10	2	7	12	3
Printing and publishing	31	23	8	26	18	8	5	5				4	9	11	2	4	1
Miscellaneous	45	26	19	32	16	16	13	10	3		1	8	13	14	7	2	

TABLE 5 (CONTINUED)
OCCUPATIONAL DISTRIBUTION OF GAINFUL WORKERS 16 YEARS OF AGE AND OVER, BY AGE, SEX AND NATIVITY, FOR STAMFORD JEWS, 1938

Occupation	All Groups			Native			Foreign Born			Nativity and Age Unknown	Age Group						
	Total	M	F	Total	M	F	Total	M	F		16-17	18-20	21-24	25-34	35-44	45-59	60 & over
Professions	193	143	50	159	112	47	34	31	3			1	33	89	53	15	2
Accountants	12	12		10	10		2	2					2	7	3		
Artists and art instructors	15	11	4	12	8	4	3	3				1	5	4	5		
Chemists	9	9		8	8		1	1					3	4	2		
Dentists	17	16	1	15	14	1	2	2						9	7	1	
Lawyers	48	47	1	37	36	1	11	11					1	19	20	8	
Physicians and surgeons	17	17		15	15		2	2						10	4	2	
Public school teachers	42	9	33	40	7	33	2	2					13	22	6	1	
Technical engineers	6	6		5	5		1	1						4	2		
Miscellaneous	27	16	11	17	9	8	10	7	3				9	10	4	3	1
Services	78	51	27	30	14	16	48	37	11			2	3	13	28	24	8
Cleaning, pressing, repairing	19	16	3	6	3	3	13	13					2	2	6	6	3
Laundries	11	8	3	4	2	2	7	6	1				1	3	4	2	1
Restaurants, ice cream parlors	15	9	6	5	3	2	10	6	4			1		3	3	7	1
Rooming houses	15	5	10	6	1	5	9	4	5					1	8	3	3
Theatres and amusements	5	4	1	2	1	1	3	3						1	3	1	
Miscellaneous	13	9	4	7	4	3	6	5	1			1		3	4	5	3
Public Service	12	8	4	12	8	4							4	4	2	2	
Public Utilities	2		2	2		2							1	1			
Unclassified	111	59	52	80	33	47	31	26	5			12	23	41	15	16	4
Occupation Unknown	106	75	31														

are owned by Jews. Of the 17 retail dry goods dealers, 10 are Jews. There are 30 dealers in women's and misses' clothes and of these 22 are Jews. Jews own also 13 of the 15 men's furnishing shops, 6 of the 10 millineries, 3 of the 6 corset shops, and 10 of the 19 shoe stores.

In the food distribution field the Jews are prominent only in the larger markets and in some branches of the wholesale trade. The five largest markets, exclusive of the chain stores, are owned by Jews. The only cattle slaughtering in Stamford for the wholesale trade is done by a Jewish firm. Only 2 wholesale produce dealers are listed and both are Jews. There are two wholesale

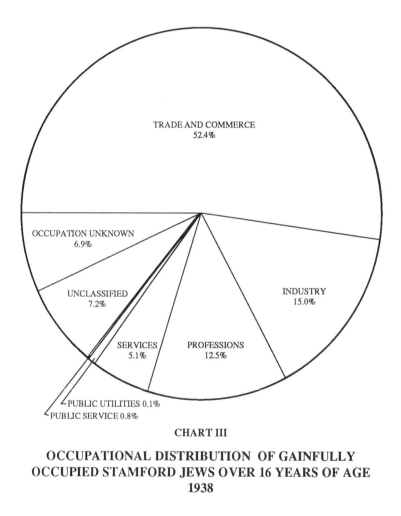

CHART III

OCCUPATIONAL DISTRIBUTION OF GAINFULLY OCCUPIED STAMFORD JEWS OVER 16 YEARS OF AGE 1938

BRAZEL'S KOSHER BUTCHER SHOP — 69 PACIFIC STREET

A Pacific Street landmark for many years. Pictured from Left to Right: Chaim Brazel, Bertha Brazel, Beatrice Brazel, Frieda Brazel, Ida Frankel, Beryl Brazel, S. Bernstein, the Schochet, or ritual slaughterer. In the 1899 city director, he was listed as "Jewish Rabbi." Photo circa 1935.

grocers of which one is a Jew. Of the three butter, egg, and cheese dealers, 2 are Jews, and of the six retail produce dealers, 3 are Jews. There are 7 wholesale meat firms, of which 3 are Jewish, and 9 delicatessen stores, of which 3 are owned by Jews. On the other hand, of the 188 retail grocery stores listed, only 23 have Jewish owners. Jews are also prominent in both the retail and wholesale liquor business. There are 18 Jewish-owned retail package stores among the 51 listed and 2 Jews among the 7 wholesale liquor dealers.

Jews practically control the jewelry business, with 13 out of a total of 15 establishments in this field. There exist 2 wholesale

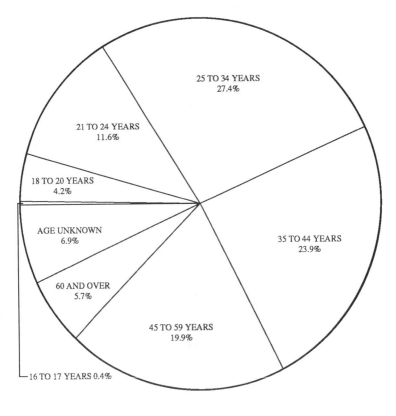

CHART IV

**AGE GROUP DISTRIBUTION OF GAINFULLY
OCCUPIED STAMFORD JEWS
1938**

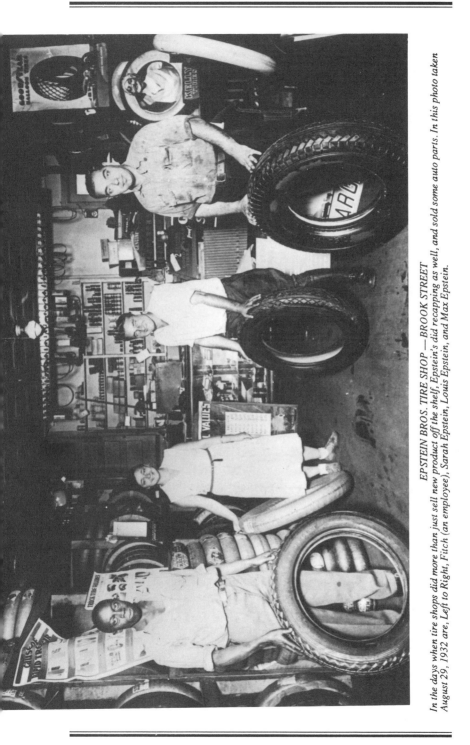

EPSTEIN BROS. TIRE SHOP — BROOK STREET

In the days when tire shops did more than just sell new product off the shelf, Epstein's did recapping as well, and sold some auto parts. In this photo taken August 29, 1932 are, Left to Right, Fitch (an employee), Sarah Epstein, Louis Epstein, and Max Epstein.

drug firms, both of which are Jewish; and 3 cut-rate cosmetic stores, of which 2 are owned by Jews. On the other hand, of the 26 druggists listed, only 9 are Jews. The Jews are also well represented in the furniture and builders' supply fields. Among the 25 furniture stores, which include radio and music shops, 14 are Jewish-owned. Jews own 6 of the 11 electrical supply stores, 4 of the 11 hardware shops, 3 of the 11 paint stores, 3 of the 5 plumbing supply firms, and 1 of the 3 lumber yards. Finally of the 7 department stores, 3 are owned by Jews. Only one of these, however, deserves the name of department store, and that is owned by a non-resident. Jews may be found, of course, in many other business fields, but in none of these are they prominent.

The role the Jews play in the financial world of the town is entirely negligible. Of the fourteen banks and financial houses listed, only two are controlled by Jews. These two, moreover, are quite small, and their place in the economic life of the town is of comparatively little importance. Similarly, the Jewish insurance and real estate agencies are far from holding a leading position in the field. Of the 85 insurance agencies 10 are controlled by Jews and of the 133 real estate agencies 18 are operated by them.

Next in importance to trade and commerce in the economic life of the Stamford Jews is industry, in which 231 individuals are engaged. The Stamford Chamber of Commerce lists, for 1938, 61 major industrial establishments in the city. Of these, 11 are owned by Jews. It should be noted, however, that most of these are non-residents and, secondly, that none of the Jewish-owned factories approaches in size or number of workers the larger establishments controlled by non-Jews. The most important Jewish-owned factories are engaged in producing women's garments, cellophane, paint, electric specialties, novelties, chemicals, and hardware. As can be seen from Table 5, however, the industry engaging the largest single group of individuals is of the non-manufacturing type, namely, building. The next largest group is engaged in the manufacture of women's clothes. This is followed closely by the hardware industry and printing and publishing. Of the other manufactures engaged in by a considerable number of Jews, only that of food products is of any importance at all.

The employment status of the Stamford Jews is clearly brought out in Table 6 and Chart V. Of the 231 individuals engaged in industry, 39 are owners, or, as in the case of the building industry, contractors. Of the remaining 192, 77 are employed in some executive capacity or as salesmen and clerks, and 115 as industrial workers. The total number of industrial workers among the Stamford Jews, which is only 136, or 8.8 per cent of the gainfully occupied, is therefore quite negligible. Moreover, those workers are not by any means concentrated, as might be expected, in the clothing industry, but are distributed among several industries, with the largest percentage in the building industry, and in the printing, office equipment, and cellophane establishments. Very few of them are unskilled, and quite a number are highly skilled.

Clothing manufacturing in Stamford is limited to women's garments. Of the eleven factories now existing in town, six are owned by Jews. Among the approximately 100 workers employed by the largest of them there are only two Jews. The next largest, with about 80 workers, has no Jewish employees, while the other

TABLE 6
EMPLOYMENT STATUS OF GAINFUL WORKERS, BY SEX, NATIVITY AND FIELD OF OCCUPATION, FOR STAMFORD JEWS, 1938

Sex, Nativity and Field of Occupation	All Groups		Self-Employed**	Wives of Self-Employed***	Executives, Foremen and Managers	Sales Clerks, Agents and Collectors	Office Workers	Industrial Workers	Professional Employees	Other Occupations	Unknown
	Number	Per cent									
Total All Fields	1,540*		597	85	59	284	132	136	93	48	106
Per Cent		100.0	38.8	5.5	3.8	18.4	8.6	8.8	6.0	3.1	6.9
Male	1,120	72.7	454		53	210	21	115	49	43	75
Female	420	27.3	43	85	6	74	111	21	44	5	31
Native	859	55.8	299	32	41	215	119	56	79	31	
Male	577	37.5	273		37	155	17	43	38	27	
Female	282	18.3	26	32	4	60	102	13	41	4	
Foreign Born	575	37.3	298	53	18	69	13	80	14	17	
Male	468	30.4	281		16	55	4	72	11	16	
Female	107	6.9	17	53	2	14	9	8	3	1	
Nativity Unknown	106	6.9									106
Trade and Commerce	807	52.4	394	75	38	228	52	11		9	
Industry	231	15.0	39	6	17	10	36	115		8	
Professions	193	12.5	100						93		
Services	78	5.1	54	4		3	4	6		7	
Public Service	12	0.8			1		5			6	
Public Utilities	2	0.1					2				
Unclassified	111	7.2	10			43	33	4		18	
Occupation Unknown	106	6.9									106

*Of these, 1,278, or 83%, are occupied in town and 156, or 10.1%, out of town.

**This category includes professionals.

***Occupied in husbands' establishments but not listed as co-owners.

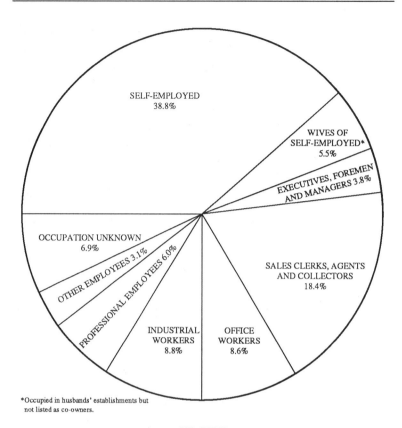

SELF-EMPLOYED
38.8%

WIVES OF
SELF-EMPLOYED*
5.5%

EXECUTIVES, FOREMEN
AND MANAGERS 3.8%

OCCUPATION UNKNOWN
6.9%

OTHER EMPLOYEES 3.1%

PROFESSIONAL EMPLOYEES 6.0%

SALES CLERKS, AGENTS
AND COLLECTORS
18.4%

INDUSTRIAL
WORKERS
8.8%

OFFICE
WORKERS
8.6%

*Occupied in husbands' establishments but
not listed as co-owners.

CHART V

**EMPLOYMENT STATUS OF GAINFULLY OCCUPIED
STAMFORD JEWS OVER 16 YEARS OF AGE
1938**

four, with 50, 40, 35 and 30 workers respectively, employ altogether 16 Jews. The dress factories owned by non-Jews give
employment to about 330 workers. Among these only two Jews
can be found. The insignificance of the number of Jewish workers
in this industry becomes even more striking when we consider
that Local 147 of the International Ladies' Garment Workers
Union, which takes in all of Fairfield County, has 23 Jewish
members, while Local 146, consisting of a membership of about
700, includes only 8 Jews.

In the printing plant of the Conde-Nast Publications, situated
outside the Stamford city limits, Jewish workers comprise about

5 per cent of the 1,200 employees, according to the employment manager. These, however, are residents not only of Stamford but of other neighboring towns, particularly Greenwich. All of them are factory workers, and only three occupy executive positions. Among the 475 workers employed by the largest office equipment factory in town, there are 25-30, and among the 250 workers in the cellophane factory there are 27 Jews. In the largest manufacturing establishment in town, the Yale and Towne hardware factory, there are a few Jews among the thousands of workers employed. Similarly, Norma Hoffman, manufacturer of bearings, has only several Jews among its hundreds of workers.{25} Of the six heads of departments, however, three are Jews. Another major factory, the Shick Dry Shaver, has only 12 Jews among its approximately 700 workers, all of whom are highly skilled. In the other large factories the number of Jewish workers is even smaller. On the other hand, in most of the establishments manufacturing products of a synthetic nature, a goodly number, and in some cases the majority, of the chemists are Jews.

The number of Jews employed in public service is most insignificant, there being twelve altogether. Among those who could not be classified as professionals there are only 6 Jews, of whom two are policemen, one a fireman, one a foreman of a road gang, one a collector of internal revenue, and one an inspector of motor vehicles. The 6 others are appointed or elected office holders from among the professions. If the 42 public school teachers, 9 of whom are employed out of town, were added to the above, the total number of Jews in public service would come up to only 54. In the public utilities, Jewish employees are practically non-existent. Of the over 1,000 employees in this field only two are known to be Jews.

Another glance at Table 5 will show that next to trade and manufacturing it is the professions that claim the largest number of all gainfully occupied Jews in Stamford. Close to two hundred, or 12.5 per cent of the total, as disclosed by Table 6, are professionals. Among the professions, it is the practice of law that takes first place. Closely following the lawyers are the school teachers. These, again, are followed, in order of numerical importance, by dentists, physicians, artists, accountants, chemists and technical engineers.

Of the 110 lawyers in Stamford 48 are Jews. Of these, it should be noted, however, only 38 are actually practicing in Stamford, the other 10 being either engaged in practice out of town or following some other pursuit. Despite their constituting such a large proportion in the profession, most of the Jewish lawyers are limited in their practice to the relatively minor aspects of the legal work in the town. Their work consists principally of general business, real estate, bankruptcy and collection cases, and some domestic and negligence litigation, with practically no share in the more lucrative cases involving probate and estate work, utilities and insurance companies, banks, large industries, etc. Their representation on the bench and in the legal branch of the city administration is also negligible. Altogether seven Jewish lawyers have held administrative positions in the City Court, and of these only one has held the position of judge; while, in the city administration, only three Jewish attorneys have held the position of Corporation or Town Counsel.[3]

Teaching, as we have noted, is another profession in which a considerable number of Jews are engaged. There are 42 public school teachers. Since 9 of them, as pointed out above, are employed in out-of-town schools, only 33 of the 419 public school teachers in town are Jewish. On the other hand, the total number of individuals engaged in teaching would be somewhat higher were we to include instructors in music, dancing, Hebrew, etc. The medical and dental professions include each 17 Jewish members. Since there are altogether 101 physicians and only 51 dentists in town, the proportion of Jews in the latter profession is, of course, much the larger. Investigation shows that there are 12 Jewish accountants, 4 of whom are engaged in out-of-town practice. The exact proportion of Jewish to non-Jewish accountants in the city was unobtainable, since the Directory lists only those maintaining regular offices. Of the 13 listed, 5 are Jews. Comparatively few Jews, as seen in Table 5, are engaged in the other professions.

The total number of Jews in the various personal services is 85. The largest group, as disclosed by Table 5, is in "cleaning, pressing, and repairing." In this category are included all the Jewish tailors who at one time would have been classified as merchant tailors. With the virtual disappearance of the tailoring trade, in which Jews once took a prominent place, those who did not go into factory work opened or got employment in cleaning and repair shops. Nine of the 36 tailoring shops and 7 of the 21 cleaning shops are operated by Jews. Of the 50 shoe repairers listed, only 2 are Jews. Jews are quite prominent as owners and operators of moving picture houses and hotels. Of the 5 motion picture theatres, 4 are operated by Jews, 3 by non-residents and 1 by a resident; and of the 3 hotels, 2 are operated by non-resident Jews. In newspaper distribution too, with four owners of newspaper routes and a goodly number of newsdealers, the Jews probably control the field. Jews are represented in practically every other service, but in none are they of much importance, except perhaps in laundering, as 2 of the 11 existing laundries are of Jewish ownership. Of the over 100 restaurants, lunch rooms and ice cream parlors, only 5 are owned by Jews; and of the 137 individuals listed as renting furnished rooms 15 are Jews.

As clearly shown in Table 6, the bulk of all the gainfully occupied work, to use a popular expression, "for themselves." Well over one third, 38.8 per cent to be exact, of those in business and industry, are self-employed or are owners of their establishments, a fact which brings out the tendency on the part of the Jews toward independence in occupation.[4] As is further shown in Table 6, 3.8 per cent of the individuals engaged in business or industry work in some executive capacity. To the latter may be added the 5.5 per cent of wives of owners, not listed as co-owners, who are occupied in their husbands' establishments — a common occurrence, particularly among the foreign-born. Another 20 per cent are either clerks, agents, collectors, or office workers, and only 8.8 per cent are what would be classified as industrial workers.

Although constituting 37.3 per cent of the total number of gainfully occupied, the foreign-born, as can be seen in Table 6, have a much larger representation in the owner class than the natives. This is undoubtedly due largely to the fact that most establishments have been founded by the foreign-born and their children have not yet taken them over. On the other hand, among the executives, i.e., those actively engaged in conducting the business, the natives outnumber the foreign-born more than 2 to 1. Similarly, among those charged with carrying on the business, sales-clerks, etc. over two thirds are native-born. It is also interesting to note that among the foreign-born the number of wives assisting in business is far greater than among the native-born. On the other hand, there are twice as many executives and about four times as many sales-clerks, among the native-born as among the foreign-born women.

The largest number of both native and foreign-born individuals in the community, as already brought out, is engaged in commerce and industry. In the field of business, well over one half, as disclosed by Table 6, are still of foreign birth. On the other hand, among those engaged in industry, the native-born slightly outnumber those of foreign birth. Upon taking another glance at Table 5 we note that in only a few cases are there any striking differences between the type of business engaged in by each group. Figures in the same Table indicate that the native-born exceed the foreign-born to the extent of 2 to 1 in the selling of automobiles and in the drug and cosmetics business. Of the 15 hucksters and peddlers, however, only one is native-born. In industry the natives exceed in number the foreign-born, but only to a very slight extent. Here, too, the occupational differentiation is striking in only a few cases. In the clothing industry the foreign-born outnumber the natives 2 to 1. The number of native-born in the building industry is also exceeded by those of foreign birth, although not to the same extent. On the other hand, the foreign-born constitute only one sixth of all engaged in printing and publishing. Comparatively few of all gainfully occupied are, as we have seen, industrial workers. Among the individuals in this class, however, the foreign-born, as shown in Table 6, again outnumber considerably those of native birth.

In the professions, the next largest occupational field, only little over one fifth are individuals of foreign birth. The relative importance of each profession as a Jewish occupation has already been discussed. What may yet be worth pointing out is that of the native professionals almost one third are women while among the foreign-born there are practically no women. The women professionals are almost all school teachers. Since individuals of foreign birth, for obvious reasons, can very seldom enter upon a school teaching career, the absence of foreign-born women in th professions is quite understandable. Finally, in the remaining occupational field of importance, services, we again encounter a larger percentage of foreign than native-born. As far as distribution among the various branches is concerned, only in "cleaning and repairing" and restaurant keeping is there a noticeable difference between the two groups. In the former the foreign-born outnumber the natives almost 2 to 1, and in the latter the exact opposite is true.

The economic structure of the Jewish community appears thus to rest largely upon commerce and industry with the professions entering as a vital part of the structure. The native-born in many cases follow the line of business of their foreign-born parents. Only in a few branches of commerce and industry, as we have seen, do the natives tend to be dominant. The native-born, for obvious reasons, are to be found in larger numbers in the professions. This peculiarity of the economic structure is no doubt largely determined by certain predispositions which in themselves are the results of peculiar circumstances and conditions, touched upon in a previous chapter.

Footnotes

1. All data contained in this chapter, except when otherwise indicated, are based on a house-to-house survey, conducted during the latter part of 1938, covering all of the 960 Jewish families in town, excepting 36, who either refused to give information or were inaccessible. In the gathering of the information, especially designed schedules were used, which, when completed, served as a basis for the accompanying tables.
2. "Foreign" and "native" being determined by the head of the family.
3. In the very early days of the Jewish settlement, as stated in a preceeding chapter, a Jewish lawyer by the name of Samuel H. Cohen held what seems to have been a temporary appointment as judge of the probate court for a period of about six months.
4. Included in these are the professions.

CHAPTER VIII

THE HOUSE THAT UNITES

Social life in the Jewish community is highly organized. The Jews found it necessary to organize extensively partly because of their own desire and partly because of the desire of others. To reduce it to simple terms, there is, on the one hand, the strong urge on the part of the Jews to preserve their cultural heritage and group life, and hence to live a life of their own, and, on the other, the unwillingness of the Gentiles to admit them into their society on equal terms. The Jews have, therefore, been forced to create a social structure that would fill the needs of their own making, so to speak, as well as those brought about by outside forces. Thus we find them attempting to order their communal life in a manner that would enable them to function as normal members of the general community but within the framework of their own group.

The social and cultural life of the Jewish community can be said to be almost entirely concentrated in one building — the Community Center. The Center is a creation of the whole Jewish community, practically every social, economic, and religious class having participated in its erection. Outside of the activities carried on by the Temple, discussed in a subsequent chapter, virtually every gathering of a social or cultural nature takes place within its walls. While some of the activities are initiated and carried out directly by the Center, others are sponsored by independent organizations which use the facilities of the building. The Center thus serves both as an organized body performing functions of its own and as a clearing house for all communal activities.

The Center came into being primarily as a result of the efforts on the part of the community leadership to obtain more effective means of perpetuating Jewish group life. What brought about the success of their endeavors, however, was the need felt by the members of the community for a place where they could express their normal urge for social contacts in an atmosphere entirely congenial to them. The chief aim of the institution appears, therefore, to be, on the one hand, to preserve the cultural heritage of the group, to foster group consciousness, to keep Jewish life intact, and, on the other, to provide the members of the community with social, educational, and recreational activities. Comparatively few of the activities, as will be seen, are of a specifically Jewish nature. Nevertheless, it is argued that since these activities are sponsored by the Jewish community and are taking place in an entirely Jewish atmosphere, they automatically become not only Jewish functions, but even lead to the preservation of Jewish group life by adapting it to the American environment. In a paper delivered on May 1, 1938, before the annual meeting of the National Jewish Welfare Board in New York City, the president of the institution said: "The Jewish will to live and to live as Jews by proper adaptation to the American environment is the principal factor of the origin of the Center in our community." And another responsible officer of the institution, in an editorial in the Center *Bulletin* of December 2, 1938, expanded on this theme in saying: "The motivating ideal behind the Jewish Center movement is the desire to perpetuate Jewish life on the highest plane...Our problem is, then, to so adapt ourselves to our environment that we can become an integral part of the every-day life around us and yet retain from our Jewish heritage those values which are essential to our survival...In the Center we do those things which it is normal for Americans to do, but we do them as Jews, in the company of our fellow Jews. A basketball game in the Center, a lecture on Spain, a current events talk, an art class, all become instruments of survival because they arouse Jewish loyalties, throw us in company with other Jews, stimulate Jewish reactions."

A great effort is continuously being made to make available to the members of the Jewish community all the social, educational, and recreational facilities usually found in the best equipped general institutions of this type. In back of this is undoubtedly the desire to make Jewish communal life as self-sufficient and as wholesome as possible, to provide for the spiritual and physical needs of the members of the community. But to some extent it is the result of a strong desire on the part of the community for general approval. Being the object of all kinds of accusations as

Jews, members of the community are particularly anxious to disprove these accusations by doing what would be expected of them as good Americans and good neighbors. This attitude is clearly expressed by the president of the institution. "The Center," he states in the above-mentioned paper, "participates in and deals directly and indirectly with many problems of a civic nature, as well as Jewish problems of national and international scope. Our Center is a member of the Stamford Community Chest, and in a current survey for the chest of the local seventeen character building and general welfare agencies made by the Community Chests and Councils, Incorporated, the Center was commended for its administrative excellence and for approaching the ideal in the development of group work, youth organizations and general objectives of a character building agency. During the last two or three years particular emphasis has been given to the stimulation of a constructive program of youth activities, and considering the large number of clubs and groups, we are satisfied that we are gradually gaining the interest of youth in the development of a consciousness which blends and harmonizes the Jewish attitudes with the best traditions of American democracy." And at another juncture in this discussion he states: "From the point of view of the non-Jewish community, the Center reflects the personality of the Jew and the totality of Jewish interests. It was told to me in the following terms by the local civic leader...'Before the Center was built, we of the non-Jewish community looked upon the Jewish people as reflected in the behavior and conduct of several of your leading Jewish citizens. Since the Center was built and placed itself in the forefront of our community as a civic, educational, and character building institution, we evaluate Jewish life, Jewish responsibility and leadership entirely in terms of what emanates from the Jewish Center.' I know that this view is not singular because I had occasion to be in direct contact with many of the non-Jewish leading citizens in the community, and I am satisfied that this is the accepted viewpoint...From the point of view of the non-Jew, Jewish integrity and responsibility in a small community can well be understood and exemplified through the Jewish Community Center."

While the Center's primary concern, indeed its *raison d'etre*, is to preserve the distinct cultural life of the Jew, its actual program of activities would seem to encourage the process of adaptation going on within the group, albeit in a manner which will leave essential Jewish cultural values intact. Whether a continuous adoption of the cultural patterns of the non-Jews — and there is no reason to believe that it will not be continuous — will eventually lead to complete cultural assimilation depends on the extent to which counteracting forces will persist. These may operate, as they actually do now, in the form of successful efforts at isolation imposed from the outside rather than the inside. For the present and undoubtedly for some time to come, "doing as Americans do" may not appear as seriously interfering with the ideal of cultural survival. To begin with, the process of adaptation has been going on only for a comparatively brief period of time. Then, too, sufficient cultural vitality remains and enough of an effort is being made by the first generation to transmit their cultural values to their offspring. Many of the activities of the Center itself aim at furthering an appreciation of the cultural heritage of the Jew and at minimizing outside influences. But resistance to the cultural impact of the non-Jewish environment in the future will probably be determined more and more by strength of the isolating forces from without.

Being a truly cooperative endeavor, the Center has on its board of directors or its various committees representatives of all major organizations functioning in the Jewish community. It was built and equipped at a cost of two hundred and five thousand dollars, and its annual budget in the past year was close to thirty thousand dollars, a considerable part of which was provided by the local Community Chest. In 1937-38, the membership reached a total of 819 of whom 630 were 20 years or over and 189 were 19 years or under. This is hardly an index to the number of people the Center serves, as all activities are open, some for a nominal fee, to every member of the community and many non-members participate in them. In charge of carrying out the activities of the Center, which are largely determined by the board of directors and its auxiliaries, is a paid executive director. Being a trained social worker with a special preparation for Jewish community work, he takes an important part in influencing policies and in initiating new projects. Although the number of second-generation young people on the board is growing, the directorship is still largely in the hands of first-generation individuals, some of whom belong to the pioneer group.

The activities of the Center may be classified as educational, cultural, social, and recreational, and are designed to provide for the needs of the child, the youth, and the adult in the community. During 1937-38 the Center maintained twenty-seven organizations, including a formal school, through which these activities have been carried on.

One of the chief objectives of the Center is to give the children of the community a formal Jewish training. We have already seen that no sooner did the community take root than provisions were made for educating the young in the religion and lore of the Jewish people. Indeed, the Hebrew school or Talmud Torah was the nucleus out of which the Hebrew Institute and its successor, the Center, evolved. The First Annual Report of the Hebrew Institute states: "It may be said that the inspiration for an Institute was created by the strongly felt need for airy, commodious, and modern classrooms in which to carry on the instruction of our children in the Hebrew language, literature, and culture. It being felt that the next important step would be to preserve the education thus acquired by them and guide them further along the path leading to healthy Judaism, there was added to the need for classrooms, a need for a place where the Jewish youth of Stamford may meet and organize into Clubs and Societies under the proper directions and receiving the proper help. And this ripened into a desire to have a cultural and Social centre for the Jews of Stamford, where through concerted action the efforts of every Jewish organization may be more successfully carried on." That the primary purpose in establishing the Center was to provide a Jewish education for the children of the community is also evident from Article 2 of its Constitution which reads: "The purposes for which said corporation is formed, are the following, to wit: to conduct, maintain, operate and manage a school for the education of boys and girls of the Jewish faith in the Hebrew language, literature and culture..." The secondary purposes mentioned in this Article are: "To conduct, maintain, operate and manage club rooms or meeting halls wherein educational, religious or benevolent society, lodge or association may meet for the transaction of its business or for the doing of any and all other acts incident to the objects and purposes of such society or association."

Although religious training formed its basis, the school early in its existence adopted a curriculum which, while not neglecting it, relegated the teaching of religion to a place secondary to the teaching of modern Hebrew and Jewish history. This emphasis upon the secular side of Jewish education was brought about at the insistence of the Zionists who were in full control of the school, and who maintained that the acquisition by the child of a knowledge of the modern Hebrew language and literature and Jewish history was even more vital to the survival of Jewish culture and aspirations than was religion. This tendency is apparent in the above-quoted article of the constitution where the teaching of "Hebrew language, literature, and culture" is made the objective of the curriculum and religion as such is not even mentioned. As if the name itself were interfering with its new aims, not only was the ancient name of heder discarded but even the more modern Talmud Torah frowned upon. Instead, *Bet-Sefer Zioni* (Zionist school) was adopted as more appropriate.

"Hebrew literature and culture" in a curriculum designed for grade school children has, of course, very limited possibilities. Consequently, what the school soon found itself attempting mainly to do was to teach the children Hebrew as a spoken language, and through it excerpts from the Bible and stories and songs of ancient and modern Jewish life, confident that it would thus bring about a revival of Hebrew as the language of conversation among the growing generation, and with it a deeper appreciation of an concern with Jewish cultural values and the aspirations of Jewish nationalism. Lacking all basis in the actual life of the American Jewish community, which is based primarily upon religious practice, these attempts gradually and almost unconsciously gave way to others concerned chiefly with giving the child a knowledge of religious beliefs and practices and preparing him for participation in the religious life of the community.

In 1938, the school, significantly named the Center Progressive Hebrew School, had an enrollment of about one hundred children of both sexes between the ages of 5 and 14. The staff consists of four instructors, one of whom also acts as principal and two of whom are only part time teachers. Two are men and two are women, and all are well qualified by training and experience to teach in this type of school. The running expenses of the school are included in the general budget of the Center. The largest part, however, is supplied by tuition fees, outright contributions by organizations, collections, and individual donations. The tuition fee per pupil is $1 a week. Children whose parents are unable to pay are admitted free, or given part scholarships. In 1937-38 the total expense of the school was $5,160, all excepting $100 going for teachers' salaries. Of this amount $1,660 was collected in tuition fees, $500 donated by the Synagogue, $1,000 contributed by the Ladies' Educational League, $198 collected on Dollar Day, and $240 received from individual donations.

The normal curriculum of such a school requires six years for graduation and 7 1/2 to 10 hours a week per class, but the school has found it impracticable to follow this schedule rigidly. The opposition of some parents to long hours, difficulties in transportation, and other factors combined to effect a considerable reduction in the hours of instruction. On the other hand, irregular enrollment and attendance brought about an abnormal division of classes. Special classes had to be instituted for late starters or to suit particular requirements of individual parents, with the result that last year the ninety-two pupils of the school had to be divided into eight extremely uneven classes. The following time and subject schedule for 1938 brings out this situation more clearly:

HEBREW SCHOOL CLASS
SCHEDULE AND CURRICULUM

Class	No. of Children	Hours/ Week	Days/ Week	Subjects
Kindergarten	16	2	1	Bible stories; Prayers; Songs; Arts and Crafts; Hebrew words used in connection with above subjects; Dramatization.
1	28	3.5	3	Hebrew Reading; Writing, and Conversation; History and Current Events; Singing.
2	11	3.5	3	Hebrew Reading; Writing, and Conversation; History and Current Events; Reading of Prayers from Siddur; Yiddish; Singing.
3-A	19	7.5	5	Hebrew; Reading of Prayers from Siddur; History and Current Events; Yiddish; Singing.
3-B	17	7.5	5	
4	11	7.5	5	Hebrew; Bible; Reading of Prayers from Siddur; History and Current Events; Yiddish; Singing.
5	9	7.5	5	Hebrew; Bible; Reading of Selections from Siddur; History and Current Events; Yiddish; Singing.
6	6	6	5	Bible (Prophets); Prayer Reading; History and Current Events; Yiddish; Singing.
Special 6	6	2	2	History and Current Events; Yiddish.

Classes are in session five days a week, Sunday to Thursday inclusively, from 4 to 7, during the regular public school year. The school is still strongly Zionist in its underlying philosophy, aiming to give its pupils an appreciation of the ideals and aspirations of Jewish nationalism through the teaching of the Hebrew language and history, and by means of stories and songs about Palestine and its past and present heroes. All of this, however, is taught to the child through the medium of the English language, Hebrew as the language of instruction having practically been given up. Attempts still continue to teach the child to converse in Hebrew and to use that language as a medium of instruction, in the hope that the child will eventually acquire enough of a speaking ability to be taught exclusively in it. But he hardly ever gets beyond the ability to speak a few sentences in Hebrew. After a while Hebrew as a medium of instruction is discarded, and the familiar sound of English is heard throughout.

Efforts are being made to utilize up-to-date educational methods. As a result, periods are set aside for drawing, or constructing out of paper, objects pertaining to Biblical or modern Palestine, dramatizations, singing, etc. The sessions, however, being very short—the total number of years spent by the average child in school is only 3 to 4 years—and the emphasis of many parents being on preparation for synagogue, these subjects do not receive the attention and time which the curriculum calls for. Hebrew history, and the Bible figure quite prominently in the curriculum, but much of the time and attention are devoted to teaching the child to read in the *siddur* (prayerbook) and to instructing him in the religious customs and ceremonies. The *bar-mitzvah* (boys' confirmation) ceremony having assumed among the American Jews an importance out of all proportion to its place in traditional Judaism, has come to require a most elaborate preparation. The school, therefore, gives considerable attention to this preparation, particularly in the higher grades, although it actually discourages parents from sending their children merely to be prepared for confirmation. And so despite all attempts to secularize it and to make it an institution for the teaching of the Hebrew language and literature and secular Jewish culture, the school concerns itself primarily with instructing the child in matters of religion.

A few words should be devoted to the place of Yiddish in the curriculum. As will be recalled, several unsuccessful attempts had been made in the past by members of the community to conduct schools with Yiddish as the medium of instruction and with the study of the language and its literature as the chief aim. Those efforts met with complete failure primarily because of ideological differences existing between the various factions within the Workmen's Circle and the split within its ranks which resulted in disagreement as to educational philosophy. Consequently, neither group could muster enough strength to maintain a school. What further accounts for the failure of these efforts is the fact that Yiddish lacks the religious sacredness and nationalistic connotation of Hebrew, and that the Yiddish school completely ignored or opposed religious instruction and substituted the philosophy of class-struggle in its stead. Since a number of parents insisted, however, that their children be taught the Yiddish language, the school was forced to include some Yiddish in its curriculum.

Despite these concessions to the various elements in the community, the time schedule and the curriculum of the school are still due for further changes. The orthodox synagogue would like to see more emphasis put on religious instruction. On the other hand, the Americanized element, particularly parents belonging to the second generation, complain that the hours of instruction are still too long, and maintain that two or three a week should be sufficient. If the wishes of this group are realized, the school may in time be forced to limit its instruction to fewer days per week and to emphasize even more the religious phase of the child's training.

In keeping with modern school methods, the program of the Center school includes extra-curricular activities designed to arouse the child's interest in the school and the lessons taught, as well as to afford him more concrete training in religious customs and ceremonies. Assemblies, Sabbath services, group celebrations or holidays, clubs, a choir, a school magazine, dramatics, and arts and crafts projects are the major extra-curricular activities.

Although the school was built to provide for the Jewish education of all the children in the community, only part of the parents giving their children such an education avail themselves of its facilities. Many, as pointed out above, insisting that the Hebrew school consumes too much of the child's time, send their children to the Temple Sunday school.[1] A few parents, moreover, prefer to have their children instructed by a private tutor. If the approximately ninety children attending Sunday school are added to the one hundred in Hebrew school and the score or so privately instructed, it is found that only about half of the total number of children of grade school age in the community receive any type of formal Jewish education. For while in 1938, 428 of the Jewish children in the community were between the ages of 5 and 13, only 228 or 53.3 per cent were enrolled in either Hebrew or Sunday school or privately tutored. This percentage is, nevertheless, more than twice as high as that for Jewish children in the United States as a whole, for a recent survey shows that only 25 per cent of them receive Jewish instruction of any kind. Of those attending Hebrew school, boys form by far the larger proportion. Out of a total enrollment of 88 in June, 1938, only 19 were girls. This can be explained on the basis of the fact that girls traditionally are not required to be confirmed or to participate actively in the religious, particularly synagogual, functions, and hence, do not need to be prepared for them. Most parents are therefore satisfied with sending their daughters to Sunday school and with whatever training that school offers.

As shown in Table 7, only about half of the children receiving Jewish instruction attend Hebrew school, the rest either attending Sunday school or being privately tutored. The bulk of those attending Hebrew school, as becomes further evident from the

TABLE 7
NUMBER AND PROPORTION OF STAMFORD JEWISH CHILDREN FROM 5 TO 13 YEARS OF AGE RECEIVING JEWISH EDUCATION, BY SEX AND BY NATIVITY OF PARENTS, 1938

Type of Instruction	All Groups			Of Foreign Parentage			Of Mixed Parentage			Of Native Parentage		
	Total	Male	Female	Total	Male	Female	Total	Male	Female	Total	Male	Female
Total Number of Children 5 to 13	428	217	211	148	74	74	111	52	59	169	91	78
Children Receiving Jewish Education	228	134	94	78	45	33	56	36	20	94	53	41
Uninstructed	200	83	117	70	29	41	55	16	39	75	38	37
Hebrew School	113	76	37	59	36	23	31	23	8	23	17	6
Religious School	93	40	53	12	3	9	19	7	12	62	30	32
Private Tutors	22	18	4	7	6	1	6	6		9	6	3
PER CENT												
Total Number of Children 5 to 13	100.0	100.0	100.0	100.0	100.0	100.0	100.0	100.0	100.0	100.0	100.0	100.0
Children Receiving Jewish Education	53.3	61.8	44.5	52.7	60.8	44.6	50.5	69.2	33.9	55.6	58.2	52.6
Uninstructed	46.7	38.2	55.5	47.3	39.2	55.4	49.5	30.8	66.1	44.4	41.7	47.4
Hebrew School	26.4	35.0	17.5	39.9	48.6	31.1	27.9	44.2	13.6	13.6	18.7	7.7
Religious School	21.7	18.4	25.1	8.1	4.1	12.2	17.1	13.5	20.3	36.7	33.0	41.0
Private Tutors	5.1	8.3	1.9	4.7	8.1	1.4	5.4	11.5		5.3	6.6	3.8

same table, are of foreign or mixed parentage, whereas the great majority of children of native parents receive Jewish instruction in Sunday school. The percentage of children attending varies with the nativity status of their parents. Of the 78 children of foreign parentage being instructed, 59 attend Hebrew school, while of the 56 children of mixed parentage less than half attend that institution, and of the 94 of native parentage less than one fourth. On the other hand, a somewhat larger proportion of children of native parentage receive Jewish instruction than of either of the two other groups.

Virtually all the children in the community, however, participate in one form or another in the activities sponsored by the Center. Those activities are designed to prepare the children for future participation in Jewish life as well as in that of the community at large. Their nature, therefore, should be an index to both the educational philosophy of the Center as well as to the interests and tendencies of the children themselves. Moreover, since children receiving or having received a Hebrew school education figure quite prominently in these activities, it will be interesting to note the extent to which the latter show the results of such an education. It undoubtedly will be still more worth noting, later on, the extent to which the activities of those belonging to a more mature age group, the majority of whom, too, are former Hebrew school pupils, could be called "Jewish" in content or aim.

All children's activities are carried on through clubs or organized groups formed by the Center. In 1937-38 there were twelve organizations of this kind functioning, with a total membership of about 450 boys and girls. Included among these is a summer home-camp. The groups containing the largest memberships were the Camp Jaysee, Center Children's Playhouse, and Center Dancing School, with 116, 111, and 49 children respectively.[2] The membership in the rest ranged between 8 and 19. While some included children of both sexes, others were either exclusively boys' or girls' groups.

The summer camp is operated on an empty wooded lot adjoining the Center building. All activities, except swimming, for which the Center pool is used, are carried on out of doors and in tents. The child spends the day and evening in "camp," being returned home at night. The number of boys and girls is about evenly divided, and their ages range between 6 and 13. Interestingly enough, a small percentage of them are non-Jewish. The regular fee per child for the five-week period is $20 to Center

A CAMP JAYSEE SWIM CLASS AT THE JEWISH CENTER — 132 PROSPECT STREET

Photo circa 1936.

members and $25 to non-members. The upkeep being naturally low, the camp manages usually to be self-supporting, sometimes even showing a small profit at the end of the season.

Directly in charge of the camp is the regular Center staff, which includes one or two of the Hebrew school teachers, and the athletic director. Adult and junior counsellors are employed to assist. The camp, according to the 1938 printed folder, is "dedicated to the physical and spiritual development of the Jewish boy or girl. Through creative activities and wholesome Jewish experiences it aims to guide the camper to the achievement of a happy, purposeful personality, and to prepare him for democratic living." More specifically, the camp "aims to bring about harmony in the mind and heart of the camper, unfolding his Jewish personality so that it may become well adjusted to the American environment and ideals." The theme of the camp, as the folder calls it, is "Democracy, Peace and Palestine," while the objectives are stated to be "Health, Joy and Education." These the camp seeks to obtain through the child's participation in the following activities: "Arts and Crafts, Badminton, Baseball, Basketball, Campfires, Dancing, Photography, Dramatics, Hikes, World Events, Singing, Trips, Nature Lore, Quiet Games, Sabbath Observance, Water Sports, Tennis, Swimming, Camp Paper, and many more." The camp activities, it is further stated, are designed to encourage "self-expression by each camper, and to provide many opportunities for his adjustment through pleasant, joyful group associations. Experiences are provided which enrich the cultural background of the child and foster healthy habits and wholesome attitudes...Campers learn the thrill and adventure of outdoor life, gathered around the campfire, in the evening; and sleeping over night in Camp Jaysee's tents.[3] Long remembered are these happy hours spent with friends and counsellors."

As becomes evident from the above description, the camp differs in no way from non-Jewish organized children's activities of this type. Its Jewishness lies mainly in the fact that its members are Jewish children and that it is directed by a Jewish staff. Of course, attempts are made to inject into activities, wherever possible, a Jewish note and even to offer the child some training of a Jewish nature, but all this is forced to the background. What naturally counts with the child is the multitude of activities going on. But the fact that all the participants in those activities as well as those directing them are Jews and that some activities receive a Jewish stamp undoubtedly has the effect of creating or extending in the child group loyalties and, particularly, group consciousness.

A similar situation prevails in the other groups. The Playhouse is really an entertainment project conducted and participated in by adults rather than by the children themselves, although children belonging to it as well as those of other Center groups do occasionally take an active part in the programs. The Playhouse is designed for children between the ages of 5 and 13. Membership in it is based on payment for a seasonal admission ticket which is fifty cents. Here again one may encounter a small number of non-Jewish children as members as well as part of the audience. The performances, taking place on Sunday afternoons during the winter months, are open to all Jewish and non-Jewish children alike upon the payment of ten cents for admission. With the exception of a *Hanukkah* and *Purim* party, in which a Biblical play, performed by the children may be included, the programs are entirely non-Jewish in content and character, consisting of the usual children's entertainment fare. Following is a typical program for the season:

1. MICHAEL AND PATTY'S PUPPETS
   Dot and Tot's adventures in the Enchanted Valley
2. CHANUKKAH PARTY AND MAGICIAN
   Prizes and refreshments
3. CIRCUS
   Tricks, animals, games — "Lots of Fun"
4. RADIO SHOW
   Station C.C.P. — Stars of the radio
5. STORY TELLERS
   Stories of many lands
6. PURIM FESTIVAL
   Amateur contest — Songs — Games — refreshments
7. CHIMPANZEE AND MUSEUM OF NATURAL HISTORY
   Know your animal friends
8. GRAND FINALE — THE PLAYHOUSE PLAY

What a show it will be! Attend the dear old C.C.P.

The song sheet of the Playhouse, distributed in mimeographed form to the children, indicates again the typically American character of the organization. These are the titles of the song: "Pussy Willow," "Through Lorraine," "Chairs to Mend," "Today is Monday," "Little Tom Tinker," "Marianina," "Cape Cod Chantey," and "Shortnin' Bread."

The Center Dancing School, which has the city's Department of Health and Recreation as co-sponsor, admits girls from 5 to 14 years of age, but conducts also a special class for children of 3 to 4. Instruction is given by a professional dancer in Tap Dancing, Ballet, Modern Ballet, and Acrobatics. The school arranges the usual recitals and occasionally participates with a number or two in the program of the Playhouse. Thus during the past season the school in a printed souvenir program announced the staging by its pupils of "Tap Interpretations." To the programs of the Playhouse it contributed "A Mother Goose Fantasy" and "The Three essentials of Dancing."

The other groups are organized in the form of clubs. Some are limited to either boys or girls and some include children of both sexes. In age the members of these clubs range 9 to 17. The organizations are sponsored and supervised by the Center staff which cooperates with the so-called Junior Activity Committee and Club Councils, whose membership is drawn from the officers of the various clubs. Of the ten clubs functioning during 1937-38, six, namely the Arcadia, Tel Hai, Tovah, Deborah, Wo-He-Lo, and Kadimah were organized primarily for social-cultural purposes, and the other four, consisting of the Sofrats, Retnecs, Maccabees and Indians, for social-athletic reasons. No better picture of the activities of these organizations could be gotten than that obtainable from the casual but vivid discussion of them by the representatives of the organizations themselves. They appear in a column entitled "Junior Club Newsettes" in the Center *Bulletin* for 1937-38.

In calling the members to activity at the beginning of the season the writer reminds them that the new club season has begun, and that "the Junior Club Committee of the Center is willing to help the clubs in all possible ways. Novel entertainments, prizes for all sorts of inter-club contest, all will make for more fun for our club members." And turning to the prospective member he asks: "Are you an important figure in your world? Are you satisfied with your social life? Come to the Center and join a club. There is one for every boy and girl, no matter what his interests are. Join a Center club and meet your old friends. Join a Center club and make new friends."

The Arcadia is the object of the following remarks: "The Arcadia is starting the season with a flourish...The club is tackling the question raised in the October issue of the *Reader's Digest:* What part have the Jews in perpetuating race prejudice? It's about time we young 'uns did a little serious thinking about problems which concern our everyday life and our place in society.

Why can't we have a public panel discussion for our parents on some of the problems and situations, which we, as thinking Jews, must face in our daily lives. Let's show our elders that we have opinions that count and that we are interested in our fate." But this seems to have been the only effort in that direction. Next we hear about the club is in connection with a novel dance arranged for Thanksgiving. The affair included a Penny-an-Inch Dance, requiring that the escort pay one cent for each inch of the girl's height, and the Big Apple. The other events arranged by the club included talks by physicians on personal hygiene, a trip to New York, and a dinner dance at "that well-known rendezvous, Rich's."

The Tel Hai program is announced to be in full swing and to include a barn dance, an inter-club ping-pong round robin, basketball games with out-of-town teams, particularly a "gigantic, super-colossal basketball game between Tel-Hai and Port Chester," climaxed by a dance to a seven piece orchestra. This society, too, had its serious moment, however, when several of its members prepared "to jump mental hurdles on the question, Resolved, That Partition of Palestine as Projected by England will be Beneficial to the Jews." This question was debated with Port Chester and the Institutional Synagogue of New York. The Kadimah, which later in the season changed its name to Crimson Flashes, announces plans for "a hilarious and fun getting meeting" at which "Professor Quizz will be there in person." Other plans call for a skating contest and social in Rye and another affair at which "there is going to be a guest speaker, bowling, and dancing.

The Tovah, Deborah, and Wo-He-Lo are the three exclusively girls' clubs. "The Deborah Girls or Debs admit any bright young thing between the ages of 14-16." They "hold a tea party on Thursday in order to overawe the new members. The gals are certainly going to town these days. At one of the last meetings the girls had an amateur hour." In another item they are referred to as "our socialites" who are going to give an open house affair with entertainment and refreshments. They also "are cooperating with the Tel Hai boys this year. With these two gangs in cahoots... there'll be swell doings, we bet." Tovah, composed of girls approximately the same age, "is going in for mental exercises with great zest...Take some drymatics, amatchur nights, mental gymnastics, and such, mix well, and season with fun, and the result is a Tovah meeting." They excel in badminton and hence "challenge any girls' club of the same age to take part in a badminton tournament." The tovah girls, it is further announced, are "in the throes of producing a play which will be bigger and better than anything heretofore given." Later on in the season "the Tovah Girls have been bitten by the Bingo Fever. They are in the midst of the throes of arranging for a Bingo party...to which guests will be invited to try their luck." It is interesting to note that these girls have recently changed their Hebrew name to Centerettes. The Wo-He-Lo (Work, Health and Love) consists of somewhat older girls. Its chief affair was a "Harold Teen" Hop, at which a member of the Wo-He-Lo Club was featured as a vocalist with one of the well known swing bands.

The Maccabees, Sofrats, Retnecs, and Judeans are all immersed in their social and athletic affairs. "The Maccabees, coached by 'Doc' Godfrey, have a swell basketball team. They guarantee to give everybody and anybody a run for their money." The Sofrats "are doing big things nowadays. They are running a raffle in order to buy new gym suits." They "are keeping up the tradition which has been theirs for the past three generations. This mighty organization will provide fun and frolic for the genus male between the ages of 13 -15." Another item states that they " are getting the wanderlust. They plan to visit noteworthy places of interest in New York." The Retnecs and Judeans, two little boys' groups, too, are busy all along with getting ready their teams for combats and with rooting for those of their brother organizations.

Frequently, under the guidance of the center staff and the Junior Club Committee, all of the these clubs cooperate in giving a play, dance, party, or other affair. Through the so-called Junior Theater Workshop, Hanukkah, Purim, or other holiday programs or plays are arranged for. These are often given an "American" flavor. Thus, in announcing a *Hamisha Assar B'Shevat* (Jewish Arbor Day) celebration, the columnist refers to it "as a swellegant soiree" and reminds the members to " practice the Big Apple...for a hilarious occasion. " The clubs also celebrate jointly such occasions as Halloween. " Halloween is here with a gallup," states the column. "All the ghosts and the goblins and witches will be revelling at the Center." Other joint get-togethers are in the form of rallies, parties, dances, and trips.

As can be seen, what primarily attracts these children are the various social, recreational, and athletic activities, carried out under the direction of a competent staff. Clubs vie with clubs, and Center teams with other local or out-of-town teams. These contests are a very important factor bringing about a closer relationship between the Jewish young people of Stamford and those of nearby communities. A considerable number of games are played with non-Jewish teams under the joint sponsorship of the community at large and some civic or minority group. This has the effects of drawing Jews and non-Jews closer together in matters of mass recreation. Another factor making for closer contact between Jews and Gentile in the community is the use of excellent Center facilities by many a civic group. The Jewish community, through its representative institution, thus becomes an active servant of the community at large — a fact in which the Jews take just pride and which the general community puts to their credit. Indeed, so active a force has the Center become in the recreational phase of the community's life that its place of leadership is generally conceded.

What sort of organizations do the children of these clubs form upon reaching a mature age? The Center has several organizations serving such young men and women. The most important and most active among them, is the so-called Center Youth Council Composed of 84 young people between the ages of 20-30, its aims are social-educational. "Encompassing" according to the Center *Bulletin* of October 3, 1937, "young men and women that truly represented our community," the activities of this organization should indeed be indicative of the interests of a large part of the young people in the Jewish community. The report in the same issue of the *Bulletin*, listing the activities for 1936-37, enumerates 17 activities, only two of which are concerned with distinctly Jewish subjects. The activities follow:

1. BEACH PARTY AND HAT TALK
2. PANEL DISCUSSION ON ANTI-SEMITISM
3. HALLOWEEN PARTY
4. REPORT OF DELEGATES SENT TO THE SOUTHERN NEW ENGLAND CONFERENCE OF THE AMERICAN YOUTH CONGRESS
5. TALK ON PAINTING
6. TALK ON THE SUPREME COURT.
7. TALK ON MUSIC
8. BOOK REVIEW
9. PRESENTATION OF THE PLAY "BURY THE DEAD" IN COOPERATION WITH THE STAMFORD LITTLE THEATER
10. SYMPOSIUM BIRO-BIDJAN AND PALESTINE
11. TEA DANCE

12. EXPERIMENTAL DANCE GROUP RECITAL
13. THEATER PARTY TO SEE "DR. FAUSTUS"
14. LECTURE ON THE EUROPEAN SCENE BY AN OFFICIAL OF THE AMERICAN LEAGUE AGAINST WAR AND FASCISM
15. VIOLIN AND PIANO RECITAL
16. BOAT RIDE
17. LECTURE ON CURRENT TRENDS IN THE DRAMA

The activities for the past season, 1937-38 show a similar tendency. These include: a dance for the benefit of the Spanish loyalists, presentation of the play: "Awake and Sing," a dance, a lecture, "How do you Dress?," a party, presentation of a skit, "How to be an Actor," an address on "Consumers' Art," a talk on "Cartoons," a review of the book Sixty Families, the sponsoring of the play "He Ain't Done Right by Nell," a talk by the city health commissioner on "Anti-Social Diseases," opera party to see "Carmen" at the Metropolitan Opera House, party to ice carnival at Madison Square Garden, dance recital by " a foremost exponent of modern dance," and a theater party to see "The Big Blow."

The other youth organizations include the Avivah, a group of girls in the late teens and early twenties, the Junior Business Club, consisting of girls working in offices, and the more recently organized Theater Workshop, Music Workshop, Journalism Workshop, and Photography Workshop. Avivah is charitable- social-educational in its aims. The nature of its activities becomes apparent from a report in the Center *Bulletin* of June 3, 1938, summarizing them for the 1937-38 season. The charitable program consisted of the Annual Benefit Bridge for the Community Chest and a Bingo Party for club members, the proceeds of which were donated to make up Thanksgiving baskets for the poor. The social program included the Annual Mother-Daughter Banquet, a talk and demonstration on "The Preparation of Bridge Delicacies," a Mock Trial, "written and participated in by club members," a program of entertainment featuring a professional magician, and the Annual Dinner Dance. The educational fare consisted of talks on "Tuberculosis" and "The Making of a Great Newspaper."

The Junior Business Club is a purely social organization, its activities being limited to giving several dances during the season. Finally, the Theater, Music, Journalism, and Photography groups aim at giving interested individuals a working knowledge in those fields, Thus the Theater Workshop announces in the March 31, 1938, issue of the *Bulletin* that "the committee in

"THE CENTER PLAYERS"

One of the dramatic groups which flourished at the Jewish Community Center, 132 Prospect Street. The Center was also a home for singing societies, craft classes, concerts, plays, lectures, and clubs of all kinds. Photo circa 1940.

charge of the scenery will begin its work to build all necessary sets for the three plays which the Center Theater Workshop is rehearsing." The plays to be presented are: "The Proposal" by Chekhov, "Relief" by Seilers, and "Return at Sunset" by Shiffrin. The other two groups, namely, those of Music and Journalism, are similarly occupied in their own fields, the former giving considerable attention to Jewish songs.

The adult activities of the Center, too, tend to assume more and more a general rather than a specifically Jewish character. This tendency undoubtedly would be much more pronounced were it not for relatively small groups of individuals, mainly of the first generation, who see to it that Jewish content is brought into the program of activities of the institution. Thus, according to the October 20, 1935, issue of the *Bulletin*, the educational program is not only designed to give every member of the Jewish community "of whatever cultural interest an opportunity to learn and study these subjects which have a particular value," but is also "arranged" as the Center cultural program folder for 1938-39 announces, by the Educational Committee as part of the Center's contribution to the cultural life of the community: The program consists of lectures and courses given by nationally famous authorities on subjects of general interest, albeit a Jewish flavor is, as a rule, brought into the discussions during the question period when the topic discussed is considered also from the Jewish point of view or in relation to Jewish life. In 1938-39 all but one of the lectures given dealt with subjects of general interest. Those were: "The World Parade," "The Jew at the Crossroads," "New Currents in American Politics," and "Where Are We Heading ?" by "an economist, journalist, and authority on investments." Of the four courses, consisting of three lectures each, again only one dealt with "Jewish Literature and Life," the others having as their topics "Significant Contemporary Drama," "Music and Our Age," and "Current American Problems," Those insisting upon "Jewishness" were thus conceded two of the eight outstanding cultural events. Aside from those, there are a few individuals who prevail on the Center leadership that a cultural program should include also some lectures in Yiddish. The program committee, therefore, usually includes three lectures in Yiddish.

Other cultural activities include weekly classes, talks by members and local leaders, discussions, symposia, concerts, recitals, etc. A considerable part of the program, as brought out subsequently, is taken up by the cultural and social affairs sponsored by the Zionist and other communal organizations housed in the Center. Attempts are perennially made to offer instruction in Yiddish, Hebrew, and Jewish literature or history, but after a short while they are given up. Few register and still fewer attend, with the result that classes of this sort usually do not go beyond the planning stage, and if they are actually started they continue to function only for part of the season. Somewhat more successful are similar efforts along general lines. The educational committee announced in the October 20, 1939, *Bulletin*, plans for offering instruction in acting and stagecraft; art including modelling and sculpture, metal and leather work, free-hand drawing, water color, etc.; modern literature, psychology, gardening, and knitting. The talks, discussions, and symposia heard are on a variety of subjects, with those of general interest outnumbering by far the ones dealing with Jewish topics. The concerts and recitals are often given by Jewish artists; but the music, songs, and dances are equally divided between those of general and Jewish content. On the other hand, recitals given by amateurs are usually exclusively non-Jewish in content. The same is true of the dramatic attempts. Every year witnesses also an art exhibit in one of the rooms of the Center. In these again works on subjects of general interest are the rule.

Activities of a social or recreational nature, many of which serve also as a means for fund-raising, are of a great variety and occupy a foremost place in the season's calendar. It is these activities that draw the crowds, that provide the real outlet for the social needs of the community, that keep the Center going. Being obliged, as heretofore stated, to move within the circle of their own group, the members of the Jewish community are actually sharing the cultural characteristics of their neighbors and are following their patterns, except that everything is taking place inside the group and that a Jewish coloring is given to the activities. The program is planned and carried out by a special Social Committee or by either of the two Center auxiliaries, the Women's Club and the Hebrew Ladies Educational League. The latter two are usually in charge of events of a fund-raising character.

No sooner does the active season start than a wealth of enthusiasm and energy are released by the members of the Social Committee and its assisting groups and individuals, all directed towards planning and carrying out a "bigger and better program than ever before." Beginning early in Fall, the season may start with tea and card parties and food and rummage sales and lead up to social hours, dinner dances, banquets, frolics, etc. The occasion for these functions may be provided by a holiday, celebration of an important event on the community's calendar, a reception tendered to a group or an individual, a charitable cause, or simply amusement. Among the holidays are included Jewish as well as non-Jewish. Halloween inspires a barn dance. In the past season, states the *Bulletin* of November 4, 1938, more than 300 people, many in costume, attended that dance, held in the large auditorium, which was transformed into a rural setting, with red lanterns replacing the usual lights and farm produce as the main decorative scheme. Similarly, New Year's is the occasion for a grand celebration of the usual type. In 1938 the party included, according to a report in the *Bulletin* for December 2, 1938 a full course dinner, music, original and artistic decorations, hats, noise makers, favors, ginger ale, etc.

Of the Jewish holidays, the jovial Purim is usually made the occasion for a celebration, which aims primarily at fund-raising, the others being celebrated by the children of the Hebrew school and organizations and clubs housed in the Center. A headline in the *Bulletin* for February 10, 1939, announces that fun was to feature the Purim frolic. In connection with the celebration of this holiday the paper states: "The plans the committee has in mind for the Auditorium will out do anything that has been seen at the Center during the previous Purim affairs. There will be enough amusement for young and old to insure an enjoyable evening. One of the new innovations will be special Palestinian and European Folk Dances, for those who wish to join in the fun. The jitterbugs of course will not be forgotten. There will be various booths of novelty games, fortune telling and refreshments of all kinds. In addition to all the attractions upstairs, there will be a basketball game in the gym between the Center Five and the Temple Emanuel Brotherhood of New York."

As the season progresses, other social events of importance take place, and are participated in by all social-minded individuals. Among these are the Annual Banquet, the Annual Dance and Card Party of the Hebrew Ladies Educational League, the Annual Bazaar and Dance, and other similar annual affairs. These are events for which elaborate preparations are made and which draw large numbers of participants. Thus the Educational League's affairs, states a report in the January 21, 1938, *Bulletin,* drew "nearly 500 people...The two auditoriums were crowded, one with dancers and the other with guests playing cards. The evening

A STAMFORD KOSHER CATERER
Rose and Abe Prushansky, Front row, Center, and their staff prepare the entree for a gala New Year's Eve Fete at the Jewish Community Center. Photo circa 1940.

proved to be an outstanding success. There were many novelty dances, one especially enjoyed being the 'Kazatzka' in which the older folks joined." An announcement in the March 31, 1939, *Bulletin* of another grand affair, named "Frisco Follies," promised the guests an evening of fun and gay entertainment, which will include "hilarious early American vaudeville acts and play, a convulsing movie of the vintage years and community singing," in an atmosphere of the gay nineties. The annual Bazaar and Dance usually closes the season, and serves therefore as a sort of grand finale. In 1938, states a report in the May 20, 1938, issue of the *Bulletin*, the affair included a Giant Bingo Game and a Popularity Contest. The other attractions announced were door awards, a terrace cafe, with "charming atmosphere" and "delicious food," and novelty games in "gayly decorated booths."

The purely recreational activities are a very important part of the Center program. Many of the members who joined the Center in the past several years, have done so because of the health and recreational opportunities which the institution provides for themselves and their families. The gymnasium, billiard room, and bowling alleys attract considerable numbers from among the members as well as outsiders. Games, matches, and tournaments of all kinds, followed by social hours and dances are arranged, and draw large crowds. Basketball games are the most popular and are played with various city and out-of-town teams, but all other types of popular sports, like softball, paddle ball, volleyball, handball, table tennis, bowling, etc., have their enthusiasts. A number of these games are climaxed by tournaments. In the past year a sports carnival on a huge scale also took place. Many neighboring communities were invited to participate in the event, which the Center plans to arrange annually. That this undertaking met with success is indicated in the following report found in the March 24, 1939, issue of the *Bulletin:* "Friendly rivalry and good fellowship marked the first sports carnival sponsored by the Center last Sunday, and the large number of out-of-town guests who attended any part of the affair went home with a feeling that they were hospitably received and well treated. Nearly 300 people attended the afternoon events, either as participants or spectators, the evening dance, or both. Between the athletic program and the social program about 150 people, mostly our guests from other Centers, enjoyed a buffet supper and later a number of them went to the pool for a mixed swim. Over 90 individuals took part in the various athletic events...Athletes from Bridgeport, Port Chester, Norwalk, New Rochelle, White Plains, Mt. Vernon and Stamford took part in the contests and games. Several other communities were represented in the large crowd that filled the auditorium for the dance."

Another annual event of importance is the so-called Annual Sports Banquet to which notables in the general sports world and civic leaders are invited. It is, indeed, intended to be a city-wide affair. Time and again, the Jewish community has elicited, as we already have noted, the praise of civic leaders as possessing a character-building institution second to none. Some of its sport events have been declared first rate and some of its teams have earned championship titles. The Jewish community, represented by the Center, rightfully looks upon itself as a leader in recreation and therefore takes particular pride in sponsoring such affairs. In describing such an event, November 12, 1937, issue of the *Bulletin* reports:..."Heading the list of notables in the sports world is the distinguished Frank Graham, New York sports writer...The affair this year in which the Jewish Center will act as host, will do honor to the great number of individuals who have won recognition in local athletic endeavors in the past year, particularly in community recreational activities sponsored by the Board of Public Recreation. The affair last year, which attracted leaders, in civic as well as sports life, was attended by over two hundred people. Invitations have been extended to managers, captains and coaches of victorious teams in every field of community recreation and it is expected that every organization will be represented."

The activities described above are only one phase of the organized life of the Jewish community. The Center, as stated at the outset of this chapter, houses practically all of the independent organizations in the community and provides facilities for their activities. Thus within the seven-months period of October 1 to May 1, 1939, states an official Center report, 66,203 persons attended the various functions or availed themselves of the facilities of the institution. Thirty-seven clubs and organizations of all kinds, continues the report, held meetings and other functions with an aggregate attendance of 10,809. Being carried on by people many of whom are members or even leaders of the institution, the activities of most of those organizations are looked upon, and rightfully so, as Center functions. Moreover, some of these organizations owe their development and successful functioning, and others their continued existence, to the excellent facilities of the Center. The Center appears, therefore, to be not only an institution having definite aims and objectives of its own, but an agency encouraging, promoting, and coordinating Jewish group life in all its aspects. In the following chapter an attempt will be made to complement the picture given here with a discussion of all those organizations and activities which, although mostly housed in the Center, are independent efforts of various groups in the community.

Footnotes:

1. As this school is, strictly speaking, an activity of the Temple, it will be discussed in connection with that institution in a subsequent chapter.
2. In 1939, certain groups were replaced by others with different names or somwhat modified aims, while some ceased functioning. Few of the groups remain constant, changes occurring all along. Here and there new efforts are started or innovations brought in; essentially, however, the aims and functions remain the same. In 1939 the Playhouse and Dancing School went out of existence and the Dramatics, Photography, and Journalism clubs were added. Jays took the place of Tovahs and Howan-Y's that of Wo-He-Lo's, etc., etc.
3. A few of the children remain overnight in the camp.

CHAPTER IX

MOVEMENTS AND ORGANIZATIONS

It can safely be said that the social and cultural life of the Stamford Jewish community is conditioned to a very large degree upon Zionism. The overwhelming majority of Jews in the community are either Zionists or in sympathy with the Zionist movement. Few are non-Zionists and still fewer are anti-Zionists. With the exception of two or three, every Jewish organization in town, no matter what its aims and objectives, is at least pro-Zionist.

Activity in behalf of the Zionist movement, as already noted began almost at the birth of the settlement. Among the pioneers there were a few individuals fired by the ideal of a reconstructed Palestine. Subordinating everything else to work for a revived Zion, they threw themselves heart and soul into the movement, preparing the soil for its eventual growth and spread in the community. As early as 1902, only five years after the first World Zionist Congress in Basle at which the movement was born, they managed to bring together a small group of settlers, and, with the help of a prominent speaker from New York, organize a Zionist society which was given the name of *"L'Maan Zion."* So untiringly and devotedly did the leaders of this organization work, so convincingly did they preach the gospel of Zionism that few in the group remained cold to their plea, and the tiny society grew in numbers and influence. Being also leaders of the group in other respects, these individuals succeeded in creating an attitude friendly to Zionism in nearly every organization and institution that was founded. Organized life in the Jewish community, therefore, became Zion-conscious, so to speak, from the very start.

Containing the most energetic individuals in the group of early settlers, *L'Maan Zion* soon became the center of life in the tiny settlement. Fiery speeches and debates, held at brief intervals, expounding the cause and arguing in its behalf won new adherents or sympathizers. Membership dues, collections, particularly on certain holidays, and fund-raising affairs kept the modest treasury filled. Members of the settlement were almost constantly approached for donations for this or for that institution or undertaking in Palestine, and, although the donations consisted of pennies rather than dollars, the sums sent in to the New York headquarters of the Zionist organization were far from insignificant, if the size and circumstances of the settlement are considered. So thorough a job did the handful of active Zionists do that in a comparatively short time they succeeded in attuning the group to Zionism. So accustomed did the members of the group become to contributing "to Palestine" that it became a habit with them — a habit which grew stronger in the course of years.

To a group already Zionistically orientated were added, immediately following the pioneer period, several immigrants who brought with them an unusual devotion to the Zionist ideal and willingness to work hard for the cause. Being of the leader type, they soon added force and vitality to the Zionist group and extended its influence in the community even farther. Work and propaganda for Zionism became intensified. The older generation was won over, and the younger, native-born generation was taught to respect and appreciate Zionist aims and aspirations. But propaganda for the cause and collecting funds for the restoration of Palestine were not the only work engaged in by the Zionists. The group took also a leading part in the building of communal institutions and organizations. As already noted, it was Zionists who were mainly responsible for founding and maintaining the Hebrew school and later the Hebrew Institute and still later the Community Center. The first president of the synagogue was a Zionist leader, and the leading members of other organized bodies were Zionists. Similarly, they provided the leadership in every important communal affair, which, consequently, received a certain Zionist hue. This widespread influence holds true today even more than in former days. The most important leaders in the community are either Zionists or Zionist sympathizers. So deeply entrenched is Zionism, as a cause, in the minds of the members of the Stamford Jewish community that to the majority a Jew and a Zionist are practically synonymous.

Zionism to some Jews, however, has come to mean little more than contributing financially towards the restoration of

Palestine and the maintenance of its institutions. To others, particularly of the first generation, it carried with it a vague nostalgic feeling. Some of them take an interest in the contemporary affairs of Palestine, rejoice in its accomplishments and are saddened by its failures, but beyond that it simply means gatherings and affairs with speakers addressing them, and, above all raising the various quotas levied upon them by headquarters. Hence, the Stamford Jew who is a Zionist finds his being one entirely compatible with his mode of individual and social life, which, as pointed out in the preceding chapter, differs little from that of the average American.

In the course of its growth, the Zionist movement experienced the usual split into right- and left-wing parties as well as a breaking up into various autonomous and semi-autonomous organizations. Accordingly, Zionist activity in Stamford is carried on by several organized bodies which differ from each other mainly in membership and the phase of Palestine endeavor emphasized. Theoretically, these parties differ in philosophy and aim, but actually the difference is far from formidable, as a number of individuals find the two wings entirely compatible and are associated with both, sometimes even as leading members. There also exists an Orthodox wing in the Zionist movement, the *"Mizrahi,"* but for one reason or another it has never been able to take root in the community.

The General Zionists form the oldest and most numerous group. They are organized in autonomous men's and women's sections, the latter going under the name of "Hadassah." Attempts at organizing the youth have resulted only in one successful, well functioning association — the Junior Hadassah, which is the counterpart of the senior organization. Numerous efforts to form other youth organizations have brought about small, short-lived clubs. In recent months a chapter of the *"Masadah,"* a national Zionist youth organization, has been established. The socialist Zionists are organized in the Jewish National Workers Alliance ("Yiddish — *Natsionaler Arbeter Farband"*) and Jewish Pioneer Women, two separate organizations having similar philosophies and aims. Finally, the Mizrahists have an organization of their own, whose existence is only nominal, as its few members remain entirely inactive.

In Stamford the men Zionists are organized at present in the so-called Louis D. Brandeis Club, which is an officially constituted branch or District of the Zionist Organization of America. Under its present name, the organization has been existing only since 1933, but its origin, as we have seen, dates back to 1902, the very beginnings of Jewish communal life in Stamford. General Zionist work was carried on at first by *L'Maan Zion,* then by the Zion Camp, and finally by the above-named club, named after the Supreme Court Justice, who at one time was head of the Zionist Organization of America. The club consists at present of 87 members, all business and professional men. Its membership includes virtually all the important communal leaders. Fully 22 members of the Board of Directors of the Center, including the president, vice-president, and all important officers, are members of the club. The rabbi, secretary, and active board members of the Temple, the president and secretary of the Synagogue, the principal and teachers of the Hebrew school are all associated with the organization, as are the most important member of the largest benefit lodge, the president of the National Workers Alliance, the secretary of the Roosevelt-Masonic Lodge, and the founder and commander of the local chapter of the Jewish War Veterans. As already indicated, at the initiative of the Club, a branch of the *Masadah* was organized in 1938 whose membership consists of 17 boys of post-high school age. Existing side by side with the Brandeis Club, but practically entirely inactive, is the old Zion Camp with only 31 members remaining in it. Being a mutual benefit society, these individuals, for obvious reasons, refuse to disband.

Although a comparatively recent outgrowth of the General Zionist organization, the Hadassah, with a membership of 232, is numerically much stronger. Organized in 1934, it is almost entirely composed of married women, wives of business and professional men. Starting in 1937 as an offshoot of the senior organization, the Junior Hadassah has a membership of 78 girls. Since a number of women were prevented from joining the Hadassah because of their inability to attend the meetings of the organization, which are usually held in the afternoon, another branch named the Business and Professional Women's Hadassah, holding its meetings in the evenings, was called into existence. Within a short period of time, the membership of this branch has grown to 51. Altogether, therefore, close to 400 women are affiliated with the Hadassah, making it the largest organization in the community.

A branch of the National Workers' Alliance was established in 1915, but ceased functioning about a year afterwards. The present organization, consisting of 78 members, had its beginning in 1928. It is a mutual benefit society including both men and women, chiefly of the small business class. The Jewish Pioneer Women branch was organized in 1936, and, as in the case of the women members of the Alliance, its 80 members are largely wives of artisans and petty storekeepers.

Zionism in the Stamford Jewish community functions thus through the medium of eight organizations. The entire membership of these organizations consists of over 600 individuals. Although nominally divided in interest, all of these organizations complement each other's work, as their aims are easily reconcilable and the ideal motivating their work is the same. The difference in philosophy dividing left from right constitutes, as pointed out, no obstacle to cooperation between the two wings, simply because the "leftists," represented by the Workers' Alliance, carry out only the general Zionist part of the party's platform, paying little or no attention to its socialist phase. The socialist Zionists, as the name implies, stand for a Palestine based on socialist principles. Their platform also calls for general socialist activity as they are affiliated with the Socialist International. In Stamford, however, the Workers' Alliance and the Pioneer Women are satisfied with emphasizing the labor phase of Palestine, i.e., concentrating upon collecting funds for workers' cooperatives and similar endeavors. What distinguishes these two organizations from the rest is the fact that they are the only ones, with the exception of the dormant *Mizrahi,* who conduct their meetings in Yiddish and, as a rule, arrange their programs in that language.

Each of the eight Zionist associations is a branch of a national organization with its own program and immediate objectives outlined for it by its respective national headquarters. They all unite in the program which has as its aim the restoration of Palestine as a Jewish National Homeland. The movement as a whole includes in its platform programs for intensive cultural activity among members and the Jewish community at large, designed to bring the Jew into a closer relationship with his spiritual homeland and its reawakening culture, but this became subordinated to fund-raising, necessitated by Palestine's increasing demands for financial support.

During the year each of the organizations has a few meetings at which speakers address the participants. These affairs are, as a rule, well attended and, being informative and inspirational, serve to keep interest in the cause alive. Now and then these organizations sponsor an activity of a purely Jewish cultural nature.

All of the Zionist organizations are not only housed in but encouraged by the Center. Their affairs form an integral part of the Center program, and the latter institution may be said to identify itself with the Zionist philosophy. Hence, to the Center activities described in the preceding chapter must be added those sponsored by the Zionist organizations. The Center becomes thus an agency for propagating the cause of Zionism, for uniting and coordinating Zionist activity. Since the activities of the Zionist Organizations are necessarily of a purely Jewish interest, they may be said to constitute one of the specifically Jewish phases of the Center's functions.

As pointed out, however, even the activities of the Zionist organizations are largely limited to the practical side of Zionism, which, when translated into action, means the raising of funds for the support of various Palestinian endeavors. In this a certain division of labor is noticeable, mostly dictated by the special interest shown by the particular organization. The Brandeis Club, which is the official branch of the general Zionist Organization of America, takes a sort of intermediary position among the organizations. Although not as active as the others, the Club nevertheless plays an important role in Zionist endeavors. The Hadassah's chief interest lies in the welfare or health phase of Palestine. Its main concentration, therefore, is upon raising funds for the building and maintaining of hospitals and for improving the health standards of the country. In this it is aided by the Junior Hadassah which has taken upon itself the support of certain branches of work of its parent organization. The National Workers' Alliance concentrates on aiding in the endeavors of the Labor Party *(Histadrut)* in Palestine. It collects funds to support the communalistic settlements and the various cooperative undertakings of the Palestine workers. Assisting it in this task is the Pioneer Women organization which is mainly concerned with the maintenance of cooperative institutions for women and children.

In the carrying on of their work the organizations are aided by the main office of the Zionist Organization of America, as well as by their respective headquarters, which supply them with speakers, lecturers, literature, and other propaganda machinery. As pointed out, some activities are carried on individually and others cooperatively. The Hadassah, both the Senior and Junior, devote most of their activities to their particular projects, as do the Alliance and Pioneer Women. But on a number of occasions all the organizations unite in certain endeavors of a general Zionist nature. The most important occasion for cooperation of all organizations, howvever, is provided by the general Zionist drive that takes place once every year. At one time there were a number of such drives every year, each seeking to raise money for a particular institution or endeavor in Palestine. In recent years, however, they were all united in one so-called United Palestine Appeal, the proceeds of which were distributed according to predetermined quotas among all the institutions and undertakings. With the refugee problem and its consequent need for aid becoming more acute, even this arrangement proved unsatisfactory. Hence in the past two years the drive has been renamed the United Jewish Appeal and has included in its solicitations funds for the aid of refugees and needy Jews all over Europe.

Stamford Jews respond readily and generously to solicitations for those funds. Contributions range from a dollar to hundreds of dollars, and few individuals or families refuse to do their share. One leading Zionist has figured out that since the formation of the first Zionist organization in Stamford in 1902 about $135,000, has been raised for Palestine, approximately $25,000 of which has been collected in the past five years. In 1938, the Stamford community contributed to the United Jewish Appeal a total of $5,400, and in 1939 a sum of approximately $12,000. A very substantial share of these amounts is usually allocated for Palestine, the rest going to the Joint Distribution Committee (an international organization of philanthropic Jews), which cares for the needy Jews in Europe, and smaller endeavors of other national organizations.

Aside from this, every organization, as already intimated, has its money raising activities, which, as a rule, do not go beyond its own membership and which are devoted to the collection of funds for the specific projects sponsored by it. These activities take the form of tea, bridge, and theater parties, luncheons, dinners, concerts, etc. The outstanding money raising event of the Hadassah is the so-called "Donor Luncheon," a yearly affair to which all those members are invited who have fulfilled their pledges of contributing a specific amount which in 1938 was eight dollars. In 1939, a report states, 250 women attended this luncheon. Other organizations have similar affairs.

In addition to raising funds, the activities sponsored by the various organizations aim, of course, to propagate the Zionist ideal. They are, therefore, by their very nature, if not always in actual content, Jewish in character and aim. Indeed, the activities of the Zionist organizations are the strongest integrating force in the Jewish community, the most significant factor in keeping

Jewish interests alive among its members. Although directly sponsored by the various organizations, they actually constitute part of the Center program. The Center includes thus among its activities a goodly number of affairs designed to arouse the interest of its members in the Zionist as well as general Jewish causes and events. Taking place in the Center and being considered part of its activities, some of these affairs are often participated in by "outsiders," while others are arranged to have a community-wide appeal. All this brings a Jewish note into the social life of the community, and undoubtedly has the effect of furthering group loyalties.

Thus the major activities of the Brandeis Club included in 1937-38 reports by delegates of the Zionist World Congress and State Convention, a lecture on Zionism by the local rabbi, a symposium by members on the Partition of Palestine, talks by out-of-town speakers on the Hebrew University and the *Masadah,* youth Zionist organization, a Palestine Bazaar and *Purim* Carnival, a luncheon meeting addressed by the former president of the Zionist Organization of America, a discussion on the British White Paper, a Passover celebration featuring a talk on Jewish humor and folklore and the singing of Jewish folk songs, and an address by the national president of *Masadah.* The Senior Hadassah's main function was the "Donor Luncheon" which, a report states, "was a gala occasion, and one that will not soon be forgotten." The program included music and dance recitals and talks on humor and youth immigration ("Youth Aliyah") to Palestine. The Junior Hadassah reports having carried out "a program of varied educational and social events. Among these were a symposium on the 'Partition of Palestine,' an address...on the condition of Jews in Poland and Western Europe, a Junior Hadassah Service at the Temple..., a party and a Spring dance." Finally the Workers' Alliance sponsored the Jewish film "Green Fields," a bridge party for the benefit of a Leon Blum colony in Palestine, *Hanukkah, Purim, Pesach,* and *Lag-B'Omer* parties, and a symposium on "Forty Years of Zionism and Forty Years of Bund."

The moving spirits in the Zionist organizations are members of the older, foreign-born generation. In some of them, however, younger, native-born individuals take a leading part. This is particularly true of the Hadassah. The senior branch is largely and the junior wholly composed of American-born women. Indeed, it has become quite fashionable among the women of the community to belong to this organization, and the membership in both branches is rapidly increasing. The Hadassahs are also the most active and, from the point of view of money raising, the most successful of the organizations. The other organizations have not succeeded in interesting the youth to organize behind them, although few of the younger people remain ignorant of or opposed to the cause or unwilling to contribute to it when called upon.

Socialism as a movement in the Jewish community has never been strong and at present is all but dead. The reason for this may be found in the general inactivity of the Socialist Party as well as in the fact that there are, as brought out in a preceding chapter, very few industrial workers among the members of the Jewish community. In 1893, a Jewish immigrant from Russia helped organize a branch of the Socialist Labor Party, which has long since ceased functioning. Throughout its short existence only two or three members of the Jewish community ever joined it. Because of the aforementioned scarcity of workers among them, the Jews of Stamford play virtually no role in the existing labor unions in town. We have already seen that in the rather large local of the International Ladies Garment Workers Union there is only a handful of Jews. Similarly, in the local Carpenters' Union, numbering several hundred members, only four Jews can be found. Only six Jews belong to the Painters' Union consisting of 120 members, and none belongs to the Plumbers' Union which has a membership of between 75 and 80.

Whatever there is of socialist activity among the Jews of Stamford, if it can be called "socialist" and "activity" at all, is concentrated in the branch of the Workmen's Circle (*"Arbeiter Ring"*), which is a national mutual aid society paying sick and death benefits and which has as its aim the propagation of the socialist doctrine among Jewish workers. Its origin in Stamford dates back to 1905, when there were a number of Jews working in the Yale and Towne hardware factory. The branch opened as #94 with 25 members who included all the Jewish Socialists and Radicals to be found in town. Being definitely anti-Zionist at the time, the Circle embarked upon activities mainly designed to counteract those of the Zionists. These activities, however, left little or no impression upon the life of the community. The organization made some attempts at constructive work but none was successful. An example of this is the effort made at conducting a school of its own, which resulted in failure, first because of the split in its ranks and secondly because of the lack of support of the rest of the members of the community.

Since the Circle, soon after is militant elements left it, fell into inactivity, betraying few signs of antagonism towards Zionist endeavors, it was welcomed to the ranks of acceptable organizations of the community. Although it did not in any way contribute to the building of the Hebrew Institute and the Center, it was recognized as a Jewish communal organization and allowed to carry on its activities in those institutions. The split in the socialist ranks, however, brought about a similar division in the Circle. As a result, the leftists seceded and established an organization of their own, which in 1930 became a branch of the International Workers' Order, a communistically orientated fraternal order. Since the Circle retained the conservative members, it was allowed, after having left the Hebrew Institute for a short period, to rejoin it and to carry on its activities in the building as heretofore, and with the completion of the Center it was permitted to use the Center building. The I.W.O. branch, on the other hand, was promptly outlawed by the community, and remains so to date. It is obliged to hold its business meetings and its few other functions in a rented room, and its members are *personae non gratae* in practically every Jewish communal institution and at their functions.

The Workmen's Circle, the representative of socialism in the community, has not been a factor of lasting importance in the life of the Stamford Jews, and at present its influence is very limited. Few of the 65 members of the organization are any longer actually workers, the great majority belonging to the small business class. Practically all of them belong to the first generation and are middle-aged or elderly individuals. Ideological differences separating them from Zionism have largely worn off in practice, if not in theory, so that some members of the Circle belong also to the National Workers' Alliance, an outspokenly Zionist organization. As intimated above, its activities are few, and are limited to business meetings and a lecture or too once a year. What keeps the organization going is its benefit phase.

The radical offshoot of the Circle, the I.W.O. branch, can hardly be considered a part of Jewish community organization, not only because the community disinherited it but because it actually maintains no connections with it. Although the I.W.O headquarters has a well-mapped-out program of cultural and propaganda activities which it urges upon the branches, the local unit does little about it. In 1930 it made an attempt to conduct a children's school, with Yiddish as the language of instruction and a curriculum in harmony with the leftist movement, but no sooner was it opened than it was forced to close down from lack of both children and funds. At present the organization consists of 43 members, mostly industrial workers and artisans. Their activities, of which little is ever heard, are confined to their own group. Very often they participate in the functions of the general branch of the I.W.O. existing in town. During the course of the year the organization manages to collect some money for "the cause." What that cause can be seen from the following allocations in 1938: $100 for the *"Morgan Freiheit"* (a Jewish communist daily published in New York); $75 for the *"Daily Worker"*; $15 for the Spanish Loyalists; $6.50 for the Hebrew Free Loan Society, which, by the way, represents its only concrete connection with a local Jewish community organization; $3.00 for the *"Yicuf,"* a Jewish cultural institution; and $3.00 for the I.W.O. school fund.

The attitude of the Jews of the town towards communists, of whom 32 are Jews, has consistently been precisely the same as that of their neighbors, namely, one of strong antagonism. From the time, moreover, that the Jewish communists were alleged to have taken an active part in provoking the Arabs against the Jews in Palestine, they began to be hated as enemies and traitors of their people. Excepting the I.W.O. branch, virtually all Jewish organizations in town are unanimous in their dislike of Jewish communists and communism in general. On this point there is even complete unanimity between the Zionists and socialists, although for somewhat different reasons. The few communists are thus excluded from full participation in Jewish communal life. The mere suspicion of having communist sympathies makes one unacceptable to practically every Jewish organization, excepting the aforementioned radical order. Recently a branch of the Young Communist League was organized, in which there are ten Jewish members. Few of these belong to any of the communal youth organizations.

Following the popular trend of labelling "red" any unorthodox movement, an organization like the League for Peace and Democracy is not exactly condemned but is certainly not welcomed by the majority of the Jewish population. One may belong to it, however, without exciting too much criticism. In Stamford the League was organized in 1938, and among its members there are 30 Jews, 15 of whom are housewives. In Stamford, as elsewhere, the League is a loosely organized society, functioning sporadically. In whatever activities it institutes, Jews take an active part.

With the exception of the Brandeis Club, The Hadassahs, and the newly organized Zionist youth society, the *Masadah,* all the organizations are also mutual aid societies, paying sick and death benefits according to the amount for which the individual and his wife or family are insured. Each of these societies functions in accordance with the tested plans of the various general insurance companies, and in compliance with the Federal and State laws. Aside from the Workmen's Circle, the Workers' Alliance, and the Jewish branch of the International Workers' Order, there are several others functioning in the community. Although these are primarily mutual benefit societies, they nevertheless take an active interest in the Zionist as well as general Jewish causes, supporting financially and morally all Jewish communal affairs. While it is mainly the concrete, financial benefits that induce an individual to belong to them and are responsible for their existence, the social factor is far from unimportant. Individuals belong to these societies because they afford them opportunities for increasing their circle of friends and acquaintances, for spending a pleasant social hour, for voicing their opinions, for rising to the leadership of a group, because of the prestige and self-esteem that may go with membership, because of the sense of belonging, and for a multitude of other reasons.

The oldest as well as the most important of these societies is the Independent Stamford Lodge with 173 members. Established in 1903 as a branch of a national order, Free Sons of Judah, it has left that order owing to financial difficulties in which the latter became involved, and, since 1911, has been organized under its present name. At present the annual dues of $10 entitle a member and his wife only to a free burial and $50 for funeral expenses. Out of the surplus, which is considerable owing to the comparatively small expense, the Lodge contributes generously to various local and national Jewish causes. The 1938 report of the lodge states that "during the past year, the Lodge has contributed $500 to the Synagogue Agudath Sholom; $200 to the Center; $120 to the United Jewish Appeal; and a scholarship to Camp Jaysee. All Jewish charitable institutions, whether local or national, have had donations given them by the Lodge."

The Independent Stamford Lodge includes in its membership some of the foremost Jewish communal leaders. As it conducts all of its meetings and affairs in the Center and has on its rolls a goodly number of Center members, it plays an important part in the organizational life of that institution. The lodge is pro-Zionist or nationalist by virtue of its membership, many of whom are Zionists or Zionist sympathizers, as well as in its professed aims. "It is the aim of this organization," states the preamble to its constitution, "to create a vast Brotherhood in our community that will embrace and reverently do homage to the spiritual achievements of the glorious past of the Jew, and subscribe to the holy aspirations which illuminate our future national life...We assert our unequivocal belief in the national renaissance of Israel saturated with a full realization of these lofty hopes and be flooded with the light of our traditional beacons." Although constituting the largest men's organization in the community, the lodge is not very active. Aside from its business meetings, which usually end with a social hour and card game, it sponsors during the year a lecture or two on a Jewish subject — last year the theme of several talks was "Democracy and Judaism" — and arranges the inevitable annual banquet and picnic.

There exist two other societies similar in their aims to the one just discussed, but little more than the shell remains of them, the days of their activity belonging entirely to the past. The one is the old Zion Camp touched upon before, and the other the Fairfield County Lodge. Ever since the establishment of the Zionist District, the Camp, which remains a branch of the national order Sons of Zion, has been in the process of disintegration. Today all that remains of the once powerful organization are twenty-one old members who meet occasionally to transact whatever business there is. The Fairfield County lodge, a branch of the national Independent Order Brith Abraham, has had a similar fate. Out of a membership that once numbered more than one hundred there remain at present only twenty old men who meet every three months and thus prevent the society from complete disintegration which would mean the loss of their insurance investments. The Independent Stamford Lodge seemingly left little room for similar organizations.

As stated before, with the exception of the Hadassahs, all of the organizations described thus far in this chapter are composed largely of individuals of the first generation. The American-born, particularly from among the younger people, join them very sparingly. Owing to certain practical considerations as well as family obligations, some of the younger people, upon being urged by their elders, joined the Stamford Lodge, but they remain there in a small minority and take little or no part in the leadership of the organization. All the lodges excepting the Fairfield County Lodge and the socialist organizations, namely, the Circle, Alliance, and I.W.O., conduct their meetings in Yiddish, although it is a

Yiddish heavily mixed with English words and expressions. On the other hand, among the other organizations mentioned there is not one which does not employ English as a medium of expression during its meetings or at other affairs.

The only organizations registering actual growth are the Hadassahs and possibly the Stamford Lodge. The Hadassahs have succeeded in attaching prestige to their organizations. Coupled with the highly charitable character of their work, this has made membership in the organizations very desirable. The result was a tremendous increase in the membership of both the senior and junior branches. The Stamford Lodge, on the other hand, owing to the practical advantages it offers, has been able not only to keep its own, but even to increase somewhat its membership. The rest of the organizations are only too happy to preserve their status quo, some, as noted, being definitely on the downward path. Few, if any, new members join them, and the prospects of new acquisitions are very dim.

A few words remain to be said regarding still another phase of organized life in the Jewish community — that concerning non-Jewish or non-sectarian organizations with which members of the community are affiliated. As pointed out in one of the preceding chapters, a number of Jews belong to general fraternal orders. Where they were welcomed or where no restrictions were put on them, they found no necessity of establishing an exclusively Jewish branch, but joined the particular organization in larger or smaller numbers. Thus, while there are very few Jewish members among the Eagles and Odd Fellows — in the latter Jews have occupied leading positions — the number of Jews in both the Elks and the Knights of Pythias is quite considerable. Indeed, the last-named lodge is predominantly Jewish. Jews occupy here the most important positions, and the affairs given by the lodge assume at times an almost entirely Jewish character. The local Lions Club, too, includes a goodly proportion of Jews among its members, three of them having been on its board of directors for a number of years. On the other hand, neither the Kiwanis nor the Rotary Club has any Jewish members. In both of these organizations membership is only by invitation, and Jews have never been invited to join.

Jewish war veterans have organized a post of their own, the Stamford Post #142 of the Jewish War Veterans of the United States, not because of any discrimination but in order to fight prejudice against Jews more effectively. Founded in 1937, the organization consists at present of 65 members and a women's auxiliary.{26} Although its chief objectives, as expressed by its founder and past president, are to propagate Americanism and democracy, "to fight bigotry wherever it is found, and to defend the rights of Jews wherever they are assailed," it takes an active part in all Jewish communal affairs and contributes to Jewish causes.

In the case of the Masons, the Jews were forced, so to speak, to establish a branch of their own, the Roosevelt Lodge, as applicants for membership in the existing lodges were consistently black-balled. The lodge was chartered in 1922 with a membership of 37. It has since increased its membership to 112, most of whom belong to the wealthier business and professional classes. Being exclusively Jewish, the lodge takes an interest in Jewish affairs and often comes to the support of Jewish institutions and causes, like the Center, the *Hachnasat Orchim,* and the United Jewish Appeal. Otherwise the organization differs in no way from other Masonic lodges. In contrast to the other organizations, the Jewish members of these non-sectarian societies are predominently American-born individuals.

CHAPTER X

RELIGION: OLD AND NEW

Religion, as we have seen, served as the basis upon which the Jewish community of Stamford was founded. As soon as there were enough settlers, permanent or temporary, to form a *minian* (ten adults gathered at prayer) services began to be held; as soon as the group was large enough the building of a synagogue was started.

Although the first settlers, and even more those who followed them, had begun to discard some of the practices of their religion prior to their coming here, they remained essentially orthodox Jews, given to the observance of the religious code of their fathers. They may have violated some precepts of their religion and disregarded others, but this was usually done "because of no choice," or because of the strong pressure of circumstances and quite "unwillingly." At any rate, the vast majority of the early settlers followed the practices of orthodox religion as much as circumstances allowed and were intent upon perpetuating them in their new home. Even though an individual was perfectly aware of his violation of certain precepts, he did not think concessions should be made, but that, on the contrary, it was possible as well as imperative to preserve the religion of his fathers in its "entirety" and "purity," and that by building the religious institution on the Old Country pattern it would thus be preserved. They naturally were aware of a changed environment and changed conditions, but never fully apprehended the implications. At most the new conditions were considered deplorable but remediable, if only the right means could be found to counteract them.

If these attempts to transplant an Old World institution in its entirety, the group was aided by the fact that there never were any West-European Jews to speak of in the community and, hence, no tendency whatever to establish a Reform synagogue. The Orthodox congregation was thus placed in the position of a Recognized Church as far as the community was concerned, and proceeded to become the center of communal activities. For a short while an unobservant person might have been led to the belief that the attempts of the group were tending toward success, that the endeavors would result in perpetuating orthodox religion, and that the synagogue here would continue to play the role that it had played in the Lithuanian or Polish town. Of course, nothing of the sort happened. Gradually, but quite consistently, one practice after another was modified observed only upon certain occasions, or entirely discarded, so that in time Orthodoxy as practiced in the European town became little more than a memory of the "good old days" cherished by a few aged individuals still clinging to it and mourning its passing.

Thus, of the approximately 960 families constituting the Jewish community, only 148 are members of the synagogue. When we consider that in 1908 fully 100 of the 150 families then making up the community belonged to the synagogue, the decrease becomes quite marked. Of course, this does not mean that only one-sixth of the families in the community remain adherents of Orthodoxy, for on certain occasions, as shown below, the synagogue is occupied to capacity by worshippers or participants in the orthodox form of ceremonies. What it does mean, however, is that, despite their adherence to some orthodox observances, the vast majority of Jews do not find it necessary to become members of the synagogue.

Of the institution of daily services little more than a trace remains. Only a few of the aged, usually retired, men, one or two transient beggars, if they happen to be in town, and the sexton observe this important feature of orthodox religion. On an ordinary weekday, only 15-20 worshippers can be found at either the morning or evening services. Very often the sexton experiences difficulty in getting together the ten adults required for those services. The practice of conducting daily services depends mostly upon the presence in the community of some mourners intent upon saying *Kaddish* (prayer for the dead), which must be done at a service with at least ten people present. On ordinary Sabbaths when no unusual event, such as a *Bar-Mitzvah,* celebration of an approaching or recent wedding, and the like, takes place, about two score of men and a score of women worshippers are present.

On such holidays as *Pesach* or *Succot,* The attendance rises to about 50-60 men and 20-30 women providing *Yizkor,* special prayer for the dead, is not said. If it is, and every major holiday has a day set aside for that prayer, the number may even be tripled. Only three times a year does the synagogue draw a capacity audience, namely, on the two days of *Rosh Hashanah* (New Year) and on *Yom Kippur* (Day of Atonement).

In the other, extra-synagogal, but nevertheless very important, observances, orthodox religion has fared about the same way. Many of the important practices have completely gone out of existence, and those that remain are followed irregularly and whenever convenient. Many of those who claim to observe the Sabbath or the holidays are satisfied with little more than attending services in the synagogue. Their shops, as a rule, are open on those days and every-day activities are carried on as usual, although some of the more strict absent themselves from their stores on Saturdays, leaving them in the hands of their children or hired help. The only day on which practically all business activity among the Jews of the community ceases is *Yom Kippur.* The institution of the ritual bath, a fundamental principle of orthodox religion, has virtually disappeared. Although a modern plunge pool (*mikvah*), was built in the rear of the synagogue at a considerable expense, only about half a dozen women make use of it. Moreover, such practices as are adhered to are observed in a haphazard fashion and quite inconsistently. Kosher meat is still bought by most of the families and the dietary laws are still observed in their homes, but individual members of the families, particularly of the younger generation, when not at home, seldom hesitate to eat non-kosher food and even forbidden meats. Furthermore, many of those who do observe certain practices admit that they are doing so not because of religious belief, but in order to perpetuate Jewish tradition, Jewish life, or for other reasons. The latter are obviously mostly rationalizations and hence show the loss of the former religious significance of those practices. The only time when these practices assume some of their former importance is in the periods of supposed or actual crises in the life of the individual. *Yom Kippur,* as already intimated, is still of serious concern to all the members of the community, because on this holiest day of the year the destiny of an individual's life in the coming year is believed to be determined. Similarly, at birth, marriage, and death one can ill afford to disregard the beliefs and practices of one's ancestors; hence the usually scrupulous observance of ceremonies on these occasions.

Despite all this, religion, as an institution, has not ceased to remain a force in the life of the community, for it is too much of a part of the culture of the group, too inextricably interwoven with its texture to disappear; it can do so only with the disappearance of a distinct group life. This being the case, it has continuously sought to perpetuate itself. In order to survive, it had to adapt itself to the existing environment and conditions. In doing so, it was forced to discard many of its original practices, change others, and adopt new ones. What has happened as a result is not that religion has been abandoned but that it has considerably changed in form. To the fundamentalist this may look like abandonment of "true" religion; to the critic of Jewish life with a certain attitude towards religion it may appear as proof of the corruption and disintegration of the institution; but to the objective observer the form religion has taken in the community must appear as an inevitable adjustment.

Although, as pointed out elsewhere, it refused to recognize changed conditions and hence opposed reforms, the orthodox synagogue was, nevertheless, forced to make concessions. But these concessions were far too slow and too inadequate to meet the ever-growing demands for a "new deal" in religion. Thus, no sanction was given to practices opposed to the orthodox creed but which were the necessary result of conditions, namely working on the Sabbath and holidays, non-attendance at services, eating of non-kosher food, etc. No allowances were made for the natural tendency of individuals to disregard practices that appeared entirely incompatible with existing circumstances. Reforms that did creep in were mainly confined, one might say, to the physical aspects of the synagogue and to methods of conducting its affairs. Thus, the present synagogue did away with the traditional platform in the center of the auditorium (*baal-emor*), and lowered and partly exposed the women's gallery (*ezrat-nashim*). Electric bulbs affixed to a bronze board bearing the names of deceased members and turned on by the sexton on the occasion of their anniversary takes the place of candles. Fees are collected and funds solicited in an up-to-date and efficient manner, and the books are kept in good order. The orthodox synagogue is, consequently, quite sound, but it has ceased to exert it s old influence and has failed to check the new trend in the religious life of the Jewish community.

The first indication of the new trend became evident with the establishment of the Sunday school, back in 1911, by the

Council of Jewish Women. The difference in opinion as to how and when the children in the community should be instructed in the religion and lore of their people presaged the coming difference in views as to how and when the God of Israel should be worshipped. The final result, as we have seen, was the establishment of another synagogue.

The broad religious reform of the German Jew could find little or no acceptance in a community composed almost entirely of Eastern European Jews and their descendants. The changes called for by the German Reform Temple were too far-reaching for Jews who only yesterday adhered to Orthodoxy. The type of reform sought by the dissenters was, therefore, so-called Conservatism. Conservatism, a comparatively recent creation of American Jews, does not eliminate any of the important tenets of orthodox Judaism, but its instituting of changes in the ritual has been erroneously taken by many of its adherents as a sanction of a degree of non-observance. Consequently, members of the conservative synagogue disregard many of the orthodox practices without feeling that they have violated any religious tenets. The innovations brought in by the Conservative Synagogue are either outright opposed to orthodox practice or at least foreign to it. The organ and choir and the sitting together of men and women are examples of the first, and the regular weekly sermon and the Sunday school are examples of the second. There is the attempt to adapt old practices to the concept of Judaism as a civilization, to give them symbolic significance, to view them as expressions of the Jewish people, of the Jewish nation. Another tendency of the conservative synagogue, undoubtedly the most consequential, is the inclusion in its program of activities that are largely social and educational in character. In stressing these, the conservative synagogue believes it has found a way of meeting the changed needs of the American Jew, a means of preserving Jewish life amidst a non-Jewish environment. Finally, the conservative synagogue, looking upon Zionism not only as the most important Jewish movement but also as one of the most potent forces in Jewish life today, has identified itself with its philosophy and has made it the basis of many of its teachings and educational activities.

At first the orthodox synagogue, opposing the trend towards reform, tried to counteract it by engaging a modern rabbi of its own — a spiritual leader who would be fully Americanized in his ways and at the same time be a strict adherent of Orthodoxy. Such a leader, it was thought, would undoubtedly inject new meaning into Orthodoxy by employing modern methods of preaching and organizing, and thus draw adherents to the orthodox synagogue. Realizing, howvever, the difficulty of turning the youth to Orthodoxy even by modern methods, the congregation discharged the rabbi after three years and decided to do without one. Henceforth the synagogue showed little activity in those fields which might have won new adherents from among the young people.

While to the orthodox-minded member of the community the movement towards reform, particularly the concrete form it acquired with the erection of the Temple building, meant desertion of the cause of "true" religion and Judaism, to the "reformer" it implied progress and enlightenment as well as saving the cause of religion by adapting it to a new set of conditions. There was also, as brought out below, the usual element of class differentiation, which entered into the problem as a minor factor in the sense that a number of individuals and families claimed social superiority and, hence, sought to dissociate themselves from the supposedly less Americanized members of the Orthodox synagogue.

In order to get an insight into what the members of the community themselves think of the establishment of the Conservative synagogue, four of their representatives, the first three active supporters of the Temple and the fourth unaffiliated with any synagogue but an important communal leader, were asked why it was necessary to break with Orthodoxy and establish a Conservative synagogue. They gave the following replies:

> All nationalities and races have their churches. Why shouldn't we have ours? The Orthodox synagogue couldn't represent us; they are old-fashioned and don't know enough about American life. We needed an institution that would be honored and respected by our neighbors.

> To redeem and retain for Jewish causes those Jews who would otherwise be entirely lost to us. To create some sort of a tie to Judaism for those Jews whose training and environment differ greatly from those of the Orthodox elements.

> We had a Jewish youth born and bred in this country, raised in an American environment, educated in American schools. What could the Orthodox synagogue offer in religion or Jewish tradition that would be intelligible and attractive to the young generation? It was obvious that an institution conducted in the language of the country, an institution to bring Jewish religion to the youth in a manner which they could understand and appreciate, was an urgent necessity.

The individual with no synagogue affiliation thought that a feeling of social superiority and the desire for ostentation were the primary factors in the establishment of the *Temple*. What the ardent member of the Orthodox synagogue would reply to such a question can easily be surmised.

The conservative congregation now claims 152 members, and a number of others who make use of the facilities of *Temple*. Like its Orthodox sister congregation, Beth-El fills all its pews only on the High Holy Days or on extraordinary occasions. There are no daily or Saturday morning services, except one for children of the higher Sunday school classes on Saturdays or an occasional *Bar-Mitzvah* (boy's confirmation) service, at which the number of those assembled varies with the size of the circle of friends and relatives of the confirmant. Friday evenings, when the main weekly services are conducted, find an average attendance of about 40, unless the service is in honor of a special occasion, such as the "Hadassah Sabbath," when the attendance is much larger. Attendance at services on important holidays is limited to about 100 worshippers, providing *Yizkor* is not being said; if it is, this number may be increased considerably or even be doubled. Exceptions to the rule are the High Holy Days and occassions like Confirmation on *Shevuoth,* Mother's Day, and Father's Day, when as many as three hundred or more may be present at the ceremonies.

In contrast to the comparative inactivity of the Orthodox synagogue where religious services are the main function, the Temple carries on a program of various activities which tend to be social, educational, or nationalistic in nature. Since these activities are conducted in the synagogue and under the leadership of the rabbi, they receive a religious character. Thus a celebration in honor of Jewish members of the high school graduating class, the Hadassah, a lodge, or any other organization or cause is automatically given a religious stamp and is looked upon as a Temple activity.

The activities of the Temple show how definite the tendency is toward adopting new ways and practices. The laxity in religious observance pointed out above, can, of course, be ascribed to a general tendency prevalent in a large part of the civilized world, but the abandonment of many of the religious practices by the Jews of the community can only be looked upon as the result of conditions unfavorable to their maintenance. The Jew cannot observe his Sabbath because it doesn't coincide with that of the dominant groups. He cannot, for the same reason, observe a host of other practices and has therefore given them up. On the other

hand, certain practices of his neighbors, being those of the dominant culture, forced themselves upon him almost unconsciously
and at times, against his will. All he had to do was to adapt them
to his own ways, and this he did. As time goes on he is becoming
more and more unaware of the fact that his ways are not his fore-
fathers' but those of his neighbors, or at most a combination of his
own and those of others. An analysis of its functions will bring
out this unmistakable tendency of the Conservative synagogue.

Thus the weekly sermon by the rabbi, a practice entirely
unessential to the ritual of the orthodox synagogue, has become
the mainstay of the Temple. The sermon is a feature of the Friday
night services, and is an essential part of them. The contents of
the sermon are not limited to religion in its credal form, but deal
with a variety of subjects which are designed to convey the thought
of Judaism as having a distinctive message concerning the vital
problems of existence, to propagate the Zionist ideal, and to incul-
cate a pride in the cultural heritage of the Jew, a feeling of group
loyalty. Often the sermon is a review of a book dealing with Jews
or Jewish life, a lecture on a phase of Jewish history, a comment
on current Jewish events, a reply to a direct or implied challenge
to Jews or religion, a discussion of a current political problem, or
anything else that may be of current interest. What should be noted,
however, is that even problems of a general character are always
discussed in their relation to Jews or the Jewish faith. Sometimes
the sermon is delivered by a guest speaker who may be a Christian.
An important source for sermon topics, too, are general civic and
national holidays, events, or celebrations, such as Mother's Day,
Father's Day, National Scout Week, and Thanksgiving, all of
which are discussed from the Jewish point of view. Following is
a list of sermons given during the 1937-38 season. In most cases
the nature of the subject discussed is quite apparent from the
title; book reviews have been indicated as such,

"An Inner Reckoning"
"Israel's Task in American Democracy"
"Shofar Calls"
"Let God In"
"What shall a Jew Live For?"
"The Brothers Ashkenazi" (Review of a book by I.J. Singer)
"Humanism through Judaism"
"Jewish Palestine"
"The Family"
"Marriage and Intermarriage"

"Dreams and Ideals"
"Judaism's Gift to Democracy"
"Saga of the Patriarchs"
"Chanukah Lights"
"Seek thy Brother"
"The Mother" (Review of Asch's novel of the same name)
"Let's Have Fun"
"Why Should Jews Survive?"
"Jesus"
"Judaism and Christianity"
"The Jewish Student" (Review of J. Dunner's novel, If I
    Forget Thee, which deals with Jewish youth in Germany)
"Ghetto Benches"
"Two Buffer States: Biro-Bidjan and Palestine"
"Tomorrow's Bread" (Review of Beatrice Bisno's novel of
    same name)
"The Jewish Genius"
"The Pharisees"
"The Religion of Youth" (in celebration of National
    Scout Week)
"The Role of Hadassah in Jewish Life"
"Silence is Suicide"
"The Buried Candelabrum" (Review of Stephen Zweig's novel)
"A Reply to an Agnostic" (Clarence Darrow)
"After Austria, What Next?"
"The Song of Songs"
"The Door of Hope"
"The Fallacy of Progress"
"The Divine Strategy"
"Zionism in American Life"
"The Jew in American Democracy" (Memorial Service in
    honor of Jewish War Veterans)
"Israel and Democracy"
"Death is No Solution" (Review of the book, Where Now
    Little Jew?)
"Converts and Proselytes"
"The American Jewish Congress"
"The Rabbis Deliberate" (Report on Central Conference of
    American Rabbis)
"Neo-Orthodoxy: Conservative and Reform Judaism"
"The Modern Version of Judaism"
"Judaism As a Civilization" (Review of M. Kaplan's book)

"God and Jewish History: Yesterday, Today and Tomorrow"
"The Mediaevil and Modern God"
"The Agnosticism of This Great Barrister" (Clarence Darrow)
"Mysticism and Jewish Education"
"Jewish Laws of Marriage and Divorce" (By Request of congregation)

The services themselves do not follow the traditional orthodox prayerbook but that adopted by the Conservative Synagogue. The content, form, and manner of worship are changed. Responsive reading in English, singing by the congregation and by guest soloists of songs from the prayerbook as well as from modern Jewish compositions, and playing on the organ of religious music occupy the most prominent place in the actual service. On important holidays, particularly on *Rosh Hashanah* and *Yom Kippur,* service follow more closely the orthodox form of worship, except that the organ is an integral part of the service — a thing unknown in the orthodox synagogue.

As already intimated, the regular religious services are only a part of the Temple's activities. It is through a number of organizations and their functions that the Temple attempts to carry out its objectives. Foremost among those organizations is the Sisterhood which with 120 members includes practically every woman member of the congregation. Its primary function is to help support the Temple and its school. This the Sisterhood does by arranging various money-raising affairs, such as bridge parties, rummage sales, food sales and the like. The Sunday school can be said to be almost completely dependent upon the Sisterhood for its maintenance. The same holds true, to a very large extent, of the other educational activities. Holiday celebrations as well as other kinds of festivities are likewise arranged and largely carried out by this organization. The Sisterhood, however, functions also as a woman's club, and as such carries on activities of a purely social or cultural character. With the exception of holiday and Sabbath parties, which will be touched upon later, the activities of the Sisterhood are not limited to those of a specifically Jewish content. Thus of four major gatherings listed below, not one, as can readily be seen, featured a Jewish subject. The main features of those four gatherings were:

1. "Is Something Wrong With Modern Youth?" (A talk by a psychologist)
2. "Current "Review" (A talk by a woman lecturer); Piano and Dance Recital" by a pianist and oriental dancer

3. Performance by a Dramatic Artist from New York
4. "Sketches from Life" by Cornelia Otis Skinner

Another outstanding organization is the Junior League. It consists of about 70 young people of both sexes, between the ages of 20 and 25. Of its nine major functions during the past season, four featured talks and five dances. The subject of discussion at one meeting was "The Jewish Contribution to Civilization"; this was followed by "Professor Quiz." The other three meetings were devoted, respectively, to a discussion of "Catholic Culture" by a Catholic priest, of "The Contribution of Protestantism" by a Protestant minister, and of "The American Way" by the local superintendent of schools, followed by the singing of Negro spirituals by a Negro choir. The dances were, respectively, a Junior League Prom ("Welcome Home" in honor of returning college students), a Winter Formal, an Informal Dance, a Valentine Day Dance, and a Summer Formal, featuring a floor show.

The Men's Club, consisting of about 25 men, is mainly educational in its objectives. Only two gatherings took place during the past season, 1937-38. One featured a talk on "Sidelights of Our Trip Abroad" by three local travelers, and the other a lecture on "The Blind Spot of Science" by an educator. The Men's Club has its counterpart in the Youth Society. Made up of about 30 youths of high-school age, the society's objectives correspond to those of its sister organization, the Junior League, namely, social-educational. Its social affairs consist of parties and dances, largely arranged by the League, and its educational activities of lectures and debates. Here, too, the program is not limited to activities of a specific Jewish character. Of the six discussions held during the past season, only two were devoted to Jewish subjects, and these were concerned with Zionism. Following are the subjects of discussion:

1. "Arabs and Jews in Palestine" (lecture)
2. "The Secrets of Science" (lecture)
3. "The Ludlow Referendum" (debate)
4. "Shall the Power of Declaring War be Taken Away From Congress and Delegated to the People of the United States? (debate)
5. "What's Behind the News?" by a local journalist (lecture)
6. "The Partition of Palestine" (debate)

A play given by the society on the occasion of *Hanukkah* under the title "The Unlighted Menorah" dealt with a religious-national subject; this was followed by a dance.

Aside from those four major organizations there exist several small children's groups: The Beth-El Girls, Boy Scouts, Girl Scouts, and Brownies. The first and last of these are little girls' groups occasionally holding a party of their own under the supervision of an adult, while the scouts are simply troops affiliated with and supervised by the general scout organizations, but using the facilities of the synagogue building.

An important place on the program of activities is given to the celebration of holidays and special occasions. These, as already pointed out, are, as a rule, planned and carried out by the Sisterhood, other organizations or groups assisting when necessary. Thus *Hanukkah* and *Purim* are celebrated by dinners usually followed by an amateur play with a Biblical theme, music recital, or other entertainment. On the occasion of Passover the Temple usually sponsors a Community *Seder, "Seder"* being the ritual supper taking place in Jewish homes on the first two nights of Passover. In this, the synagogue follows the practice of the Reform Temple whose members usually do not celebrate the holiday in their homes. Jewish Arbor Day is usually celebrated by a party featuring a talk befitting the occassion. That some of the civic and national holidays are also celebrated in the accepted manner has already been pointed out. Finally, there are the recurring anniversary dinners and installation banquets, which are considered very important functions.

The educational work of the Temple is mainly confined to the children of the members, but attempts to offer instruction to adult members of the congregation, particularly women, are constantly made by the rabbi. Thus, there exist classes in Jewish history and literature, Bible, Hebrew, and Jewish music, but they attract only a small percentage of the Temple membership. The main concentration is upon the Religious or Sunday school. With a registration of approximately eighty children between the ages of 4 1/2 and 16 and divided into a kindergarten class and eight grades, it follows the general pattern of the American Sunday school. The Bible, or rather Biblical story books, entirely excluding, of course, the New Testament, is the point of concentration. Palestine, next in attention, is the Holy Land of the Jews, and is, moreover, the country which the Jews are returning to and aspire to make their own. Present-day aspects of the country and its people, as viewed by Zionism, are therefore emphasized. Similarly do Hebrew reading, post-Biblical history, and Jewish current events occupy space in the curriculum. Where the school differs from the general Sunday school is in the teaching of religious tenets, laws, and customs which are those of the Jews instead of those of Protestants and Catholics. The actual curriculum of the school, given below, brings this out more clearly.

SUNDAY SCHOOL CURRICULUM

KINDERGARTEN AND FIRST GRADE (120 minutes)

Customs and ceremonies of the Jewish Sabbath and holidays given in the form of projects; Bible stories, folk tales, and legends selected to build up the imaginative life of the child, or to illustrate definite religious concepts, such as Sabbath, Charity, Hospitality, love for Torah, etc.; Assembly; Appropriate games, songs, prayers, dramatization, pantomime, handiwork and art work.

SECOND AND THIRD GRADES (120 minutes)

Bible — "Readings in class from Bildersee's Genesis and Out of the House of Bondage; Stories and Legends — Jewish heroes from post-Biblical times to the present; Jewish History — the story of Israel from its early origin through Moses; Customs and Ceremonies — Jewish marriage and ceremonial objects of a Jewish home; Hebrew — elements of Hebrew reading; Assembly.

FOURTH GRADE (120 minutes)

Jewish History — conquest of Canaan to the Restoration; Bible — selected chapters from the Prophets; Customs and Ceremonies Project — Jewish children in other lands; Hebrew — elements of Hebrew reading, limited Hebrew conversation, understanding of simple Hebrew prayers; Assembly.

FIFTH GRADE (120 minutes)

Jewish History — from close of the Babylonian Exile to "the period when Judaism gave religion to the Western World"; Jewish Literature — selections from the Psalms, Proverbs, Ruth, Esther, and Maccabees; Customs and Ceremonies Project — the Temple in Jewish life and synagogal objects; Hebrew — order of service, reading of principal prayers, limited Hebrew conversation; Current Events — twice a month; Assembly.

SIXTH GRADE (120 minutes)

Jewish history — from the disintegration of the Jewish state to the end of the Golden Age in Spain; Jewish Literature — selections from Jewish post-Biblical literature (Apocrypha, Midrash, Talmud, and religious poetry); Customs and Ceremonies Project — the history of prayers; Current events — twice a month; Hebrew — reading and analysis of principal Hebrew prayers; Assembly.

SEVENTH GRADE (195 minutes: Sunday, 10-12;
Saturday, 9:45-11)
Jewish history — from the days of the Middle Ages through
emancipation; Jewish Literature — readings form the Ethics
of the Fathers; Current Events — bi-weekly; Religion and
Ethics — survey of Jewish religious life; Hebrew — reading
and analysis of principal prayers of Saturday morning service; Sabbath Morning Service; Assembly.

EIGHTH GRADE (195 minutes: Sunday, 10-12; Saturday, 9:45-11)
Jewish History — from the days of emancipation to contemporary life, history of the Jews in America; Jewish Literature — selections from modern and contemporary Hebrew
literature; Jewish Religion — story of comparative religion,
preparation for confirmation; Customs and Ceremonies —
the Jewish calendar; Current Events — bi-weekly; Hebrew
— Sabbath and festival prayers; Sabbath Morning Service;
Assembly.

Classes meet on Sunday mornings between 10-12, except
during the summer. Children of the two highest grades and those
preparing for bar mitzvah are required to attend also on Saturday
mornings from 9:45-11. The teachers are either Jewish public-
school teachers or other young women or men qualified to teach.
Extra-curricular activities consist of holiday celebrations which
may include an appropriate play given by the children, movies of
Biblical or present-day Palestine, or the like, in addition to a talk
by the rabbi, explaining the significance of the occasion, and delicacies distributed by the Sisterhood. Those activities also include
picnics with athletic games, as the main attraction, visits to points
of interest such as the Metropolitan Museum of Art and Radio
City, and participation in Jewish as well as non-Jewish fund-raising campaigns like the Jewish National Fund and the Red Cross.
Graduation and Confirmation exercises — the latter introduced
into American Jewish life by the Reform and Conservative synagogues — take place at about the same time and in about the
same manner as those in non-Jewish religious schools.

The functions of the rabbi of the congregation are quite evident from what has been described above. In addition to conducting services, preaching, and initiating and conducting the aforementioned synagogal activities, he is active as a leader and
spokesman of the Jewish community. Expressing the desire of his
congregation as well as of the community as a whole, he seeks to
establish as close and as friendly a relationship as possible with
the Christian denominations. He, therefore, invites Christian

ministers and priests to address his congregation or synagogal groups, and plays an important role in the so-called inter-faith or good will movement.

To summarize, the institution of religion as existing at present in the Jewish community is gradually but steadily moving away from its traditional pattern and tending to adapt itself more and more to the exigencies of its new environment. It is giving more emphasis to the social and cultural phases of its activities. The orthodox synagogue still fills a religious need in the life of many individuals, particularly on certain occasions. Older, foreign-born individuals, even if they be ardent members of the Temple, still turn to the Synagogue on such occasions as *kaddish, yizkor,* and the like. There are cases of persons leaving the Temple in the midst of the service to attend the yizkor service in the Synagogue. But its influence hardly reaches beyond the purely religious phase of the community's life. The Temple, being an adaptation to the American scene, satisfies not only the religious but also the social needs of the members of the Jewish community. The social life of the Jewish community is still more or less isolated; Jews are still obliged to turn to their own group for many of their social contacts. The Temple has thus become one of the outlets for the social life of at least a part of the Jews of the community. It differs from the Community Center only in having a definitely religious side to it and in serving as an agency for a limited number of the members of the community — selected mainly on the basis of economic and social grouping.

The Orthodox synagogue was built by and receives its moral support from first generation immigrants — an element which is gradually disappearing. It has lost much of its appeal to the younger generation. It is true that on *Rosh Hashanah* and *Yom Kippur* or on other serious occasions second-generation individuals will still attend services in the Synagogue, but this is only because of their clinging to the old cultural patterns which they absorbed in their homes as children but which they find difficult to transmit to their offspring. What is evident, therefore, is that the orthodox synagogue is constantly losing ground. The Temple, to be sure, was also built by direct immigrants but its membership is fast becoming predominantly native-born. Its destiny is at least tied up with the younger generation. Whether the form in which it attempts to preserve the religious life of the community will succeed is, of course, impossible to answer. This depends upon the future cultural configuration of Jewish life in America of which the community under discussion is a component part.

TABLE 8

AFFILIATION OF STAMFORD JEWISH FAMILIES WITH RELIGIOUS INSTITUTIONS, BY NATIVITY OF HEAD, 1938

Nativity	All Families	Total	Membership in Religious Institution					
			Orthodox		Conservative		Members in Both	
			Number	Per Cent	Number	Per Cent	Number	Per Cent
All Groups	960	273	121	12.6	125	13.0	27	2.8
Foreign Born	528	152	92	17.4	47	8.9	13	2.5
Native	396	119	29	7,3	76	19.2	14	3.5
Unknown	36	2	2					

As to the persistence of religion in general, i.e., institutionalized religion, in the Jewish community, the above facts would seem to indicate that the vast majority of individuals are still adherents of it, even though this adherence be an occasional and a not too serious one. Some one coined the term "Yom Kippur Jews," which could be very appropriately applied to most of the members of the community. By the same token some could be termed *"Kaddish Jews,"* and *"Yizkor Jews,"* but this very fact seems to show that religious feeling is far from having disappeared and only lies dormant, coming to life when occasion calls for it. Thus, as shown in Table 8, while only 273, or 28.4 per cent, of the 960 families belong to either the Orthodox or Conservative synagogue, on *Yom Kippur* practically the whole community turns out at services. In membership both synagogues are about equally divided. As seen in the same table, among the foreign-born, about twice as many belong to the Orthodox as to the Conservative synagogue. On the other hand, among the native born, considerably over twice as many are affiliated with the Conservative as with the Orthodox synagogue. A small number are members in both. Only a comparatively few among the intellectuals and radicals show a consistent disregard of the institution and its ceremonies.

CHAPTER XI

JEWS AS MEMBERS OF THE COMMUNITY AT LARGE

For only a very short period after the establishment of the settlement did the Jews of Stamford tend to concentrate in one section of the town. As soon as their status became a more permanent one, those who could afford it moved to better neighborhoods, at first usually close by old quarters, and later to some of the best residential sections and suburbs of the town. Today there is no section in town which could properly be designated as Jewish, although a few streets, or rather parts of streets, show a slight concentration of Jewish residences. On the other hand, there are few sections where Jews do not live. Even the three Jewish community buildings, the two synagogues and the Center, are located in two of the finest sections in the city. A section of Pacific Street, where the Jews concentrated in the early days of the settlement, is still considered Jewish in character, not because of its Jewish residences — very few Jews live there at present — but because a goodly number of shops catering to the Jewish trade are located there. In this street are to be found the Jewish butcher shops, restaurant, and stores owned by old-time Jewish tradesmen who conduct their business on a small scale and on a somewhat intimate basis. The section is narrow and very short, and is the only one in town having any resemblance at all to a Ghetto street.

Probably more than any other recent immigrant group in town, the Jews have sought to become citizens of their adopted country. This is shown by the extremely low number of aliens among them. As disclosed by Table 9, of a total of 971 foreign-born individuals twenty-one years of age and over, only 98 or 10.1 per cent are not citizens or declarants. Since 11 of these have not been here long enough to qualify, the actual number is even smaller. During the World War, the Jewish community, consisting then of about 1,700 souls, sent 96, or over 4 per cent of its total number, to the armed forces and contributed almost 8 per cent of those who died in the service. The response to the various Liberty Loans was also very generous. The Stamford Jews identify themselves with the culture surrounding them. We have seen that

TABLE 9

CITIZENSHIP STATUS OF STAMFORD FOREIGN BORN JEWS 21 YEARS OF AGE AND OVER, ACCORDING TO YEARS OF RESIDENCE IN UNITED STATES, BY SEX, 1938

Years In United States	All Classes				Citizens			Declarants			Aliens		
	Total		Male	Female	Total	Male	Female	Total	Male	Female	Total	Male	Female
	No.	P.C.											
All Groups	971		514	457	862	474	388	11	7	4	98	34	64
Per Cent		100.0	52.9	47.1	88.8	48.8	40.0	1.1	0.7	0.4	10.1	3.5	6.6
Under 5 Years	15	1.5	9	6				4	3	1	11	6	3
5–10 Years	13	1.3	6	7	10	6	4				3		5
11–15 Years	24	2.5	9	15	19	9	10	1		1	4		4
16–20 Years	56	5.8	32	24	47	28	19				9	4	5
21–25 Years	101	10.4	59	42	84	51	33	2	2		15	6	9
26–30 Years	218	22.5	113	105	197	105	92				21	8	13
31–35 Years	261	26.9	134	127	237	126	111	2	1	1	22	7	15
36–40 Years	136	14.0	70	66	126	67	59	1		1	9	3	6
41–45 Years	60	6.2	31	29	57	31	26	1	1		2		2
46–50 Years	49	5.0	30	19	47	30	17				2		2
Over 50 Years	30	3.1	17	13	30	17	13						
Unknown	8	0.8	4	4	8	4	4						

their social life is essentially the same as that of their neighbors. This is also true of their home life, which is conditioned upon the prevailing customs and mores, modified slightly here and there by former cultural peculiarities. Their interests differ in no way from those of their neighbors, except that they may also include others pertaining to their own group. This is, of course, most true of the younger, American-born generation.

The language the immigrants brought with them, Yiddish, is rapidly losing ground as a medium of daily conversation even among the older, foreign-born individuals, An inquiry, covering all but thirty-six of the families, showed that there was not a single Jewish home where Yiddish was spoken exclusively. As is apparent from Table 10, in most homes where the heads of the family are of foreign birth, Yiddish is used alongside with English. The extent to which Yiddish is spoken in such households is hard to determine. The native-born members usually understand the language, but speak it occasionally and then very sparingly, when conversing with their elders. In a considerable number of such homes, as further brought out in the same table, Yiddish is not used at all. On the other hand, in the vast majority of homes where the head of the family is native-born, English is used exclusively. Only 88 out of a total of 396 of such households were found to be bi-lingual. What probably accounts for the bi-lingualism in these homes is the fact that either the mother, or some other relative who is a member of the family, may be of foreign birth and Yiddish speaking, just as the complete discard of Yiddish in households whose head is foregn-born may be due partly to the other parent being American-born. It is further noteworthy that ever fewer individuals of foreign birth claim Yiddish as their mother tongue. Thus in 1930, 44.5 per cent less individuals reported Yiddish as their mother tongue than in 1920, despite the appreciable increase in the number of foreign-born among the Stamford Jews during that decade. In 1920, the United States Census reports 1,391 and in 1930, 772 persons giving Yiddish as their mother tongue.

TABLE 10
LANGUAGE SPOKEN IN HOMES OF STAMFORD JEWS,
ACCORDING TO NATIVITY OF HEAD OF FAMILY, 1938

Nativity	Total	Yiddish and English		English Only*		Unknown	
		Number	Per Cent	Number	Per Cent	Number	Per Cent
All Families	960	498	51.0	426	44.4	36	3.7
Foreign Born	528	410	77.7	118	22.3		
Native	396	88	22.2	308	77.8		
Unknown	36						

*In this classification there are 7 families who speak German and English at home.

It may safely be said that none of the native-born individuals have recourse to the Yiddish newspapers and periodicals and that very few of them read Jewish publications printed in English. The number of individuals subscribing to Yiddish as well as Anglo-Jewish papers is far from negligible, but most of them are foreign born. Slightly more individuals subscribe to Yiddish than Anglo-Jewish publications. As can be seen in Table 11, of the 506 subscribers, 263 subscribe to Yiddish, 239 to Anglo-Jewish, and only 4 to Hebrew publications. More people subscribe to periodicals than to dailies. As might be expected, Zionist publications have three times as many subscribers as socialist ones, while only a very small fraction, 29, subscribe to the radically orientated papers. It is also worth noting that while almost two-thirds of the readers of Zionist publications subscribe to papers and periodicals printed in English, all those reading socialist or radical publications subscribe to papers printed in Yiddish. As shown in the same table, the Zionist publications subscribed to show a greater variety than either the socialist or radical. Indeed all, excepting 12, of the 112 readers of socialist papers subscribe to the *Daily Forward,* which is not a socialist party organ but socialist in orientation.

TABLE 11
NUMBER OF STAMFORD JEWS SUBSCRIBING TO JEWISH DAILIES AND PERIODICALS, BY LANGUAGE AND POLITICAL ORIENTATION OF PUBLICATION, 1938

Political Orientation of Publication	Subscribers:							Publications:						
	Total Number	English		Yiddish		Hebrew		Total Number	English		Yiddish		Hebrew	
		Dailies	Periodicals	Dailies	Periodicals	Dailies	Periodicals		Dailies	Periodicals	Dailies	Periodicals	Dailies	Periodicals
Totals	506	0	239	206	57	1	3	19	0	5	4	8	1	3
Zionist	365	0	239	91	31	1	3	11	0	5	2	2	1	3
Socialist	112	0	0	100	12	0	0	3	0	0	1	2	0	0
Radical	29	0	0	15	14	0	0	5	0	0	1	4	0	0

Relations between Jew and non-Jew in the community are friendly and cordial but usually of the non-intimate type. The gap dividing the two, however, is becoming, as pointed out before, narrower, and cases of greatest intimacy in relationship between Jew and Gentile, namely, marriage are not unusual at all. The data gathered on the frequency of intermarriage are incomplete and sketchy, owing to the obvious difficulty of obtaining information of this kind. Some idea of it, however, may be obtained from the facts given below.

Since it was impossible to get data for a period of years, the rate of intermarriage could not be obtained. Careful investigation brought out the fact that in 1938 there were 59 Jewish-Gentile families living in town. In 40 cases the Jews marrying Gentiles were men. This number of intermarriages is probably an underestimate, particularly in the case of the women, concerning whom data were less obtainable. As the census taken of the Jewish population of Stamford shows that there are 823 married couples, the 59 known Jewish-Gentile couples, which are included among them, constitute 7.2 per cent of the total. To put it on the basis of individuals, since there are altogether 1,587 married persons in the Jewish community, the 59 married to non-Jews make up 3.7 per cent of the total number of married persons.

In only 31 of the 59 cases, 18 of whom were males and 13 females, was it possible to obtain some information regarding the nature of the intermarriage. But even in these cases the information desired was not always elicited. As a result some of the observations have to be based on fewer than the thirty-one cases.

In all but five of the total number of intermarriages is the ethnic origin of the Gentile mates known. Of the seven groups represented, the Italians come first. Fully 13 of the 36 Jewish males and 8 of the 18 Jewish females are married to Italians. The Irish come next, as 12 of the men and 4 of the women have mates from among this group. Following the Irish are the Old Americans, or Yankees, from among whom 5 men and 3 women have chosen their wives and husbands respectively. Of the rest of the 36 Jewish men, two married Polish women, two Germans, and one a Czech woman; and of the remainder of the 18 Jewish women, one married a German, one a Czech, and one a Hungarian. All but 4 of the 25 individuals who replied to the question married Catholics.

All but three of the thirty-one individuals married to non-Jews were born in this country, and all except one, whose mother only was born in the United States, are of foreign-born parentage. Again, all except three of the individuals were reared by parents affiliated with a synagogue which they attended regularly or on holidays. In 25 cases out of the 31, the parents belonged to the Orthodox and in 3 to the Conservative synagogue; only in 3 cases were the parents unaffiliated with any synagogue. Economically, practically as many parents belonged to the lower as to the middle income group; only three were from among the wealthier class. The parents of the individuals were drawn from almost every occupation engaged in by the Jews of the town, except the professions. The great majority of them, twenty-one out of the twenty-seven who replied to the question, lived among and associated with Jews, and only nine of the total of thirty-one were not affiliated with any secular Jewish organization. On the other hand, ten were active members in the Orthodox synagogue and two leading Zionists. Represented among the parents whose children intermarried were also several of the old settlers who have taken a leading part in the building of the community and in Jewish communal life in general.

In twelve of the thirty-one cases the individuals married to non-Jews received a Jewish education in a Hebrew school. Thirteen of the eighteen males who replied to the question were confirmed in the synagogue (became *Bar-Mitsvah*). In the great majority of cases, 26 out of 31, the parents were aware of the courtship. That most of them disapproved of their children's marrying outside their group can be seen from the fact that 21 out of the 28 individuals from whom replies were obtained married without parental consent and without their parents being present at the wedding. It is noteworthy that in all except one of the seven instances of parent-approved intermarriages it was a case of Jewish men marrying non-Jewish women. One of the parents was a communist, one a Zionist, two avowed "assimilationists," and the other three of unknown attitudes. In all but one of the thirty-one cases, the marriage was performed by the justice of the peace only. In the one case where the couple also went through a religious ceremony, the bride, an Irish Catholic, embraced the Jewish faith, and the wedding was performed by a rabbi.

The majority of the Jewish men and women who married non-Jews continue to be regarded as members of the Jewish community, some of them keeping up their affiliation with it and taking an active part in its affairs. Only in six out of the thirty-one cases have the individuals severed all their connections with Jewish life. Nine of the thirty-one are members of either the Synagogue or the Temple. Most of them, however, are indifferent to their own as well as their mates' faith, attending neither synagogue nor church. The same is also largely true of the Gentile men and women married to Jews. Only in two cases are Jews, married to Gentiles, known to have adopted Christianity and to be affiliated with a Christian church.

The average duration of marriage as shown in 54 out of the 59 cases was, at the time of this investigation, 1938, ten and a half years in the case of men and eight and a half in the case of women. Only 14 of the 31 couples have children, and only two of these have more than one child. In six cases the children receive no religious training whatever, in five they are reared as Jews, and in three as Christians.

The Stamford Jews have made significant contributions to the economic development of the town. Many a business and industrial enterprise is directly traceable to their initiative and effort. It was a Jewish citizen, an immigrant from Poland, who was mainly responsible for the development of Atlantic Street into the foremost business street.{27} Some of the most important civic buildings, such as the Town Hall, Stamford Hospital, Ferguson Public Library and Firehouse were also built by him. A Jewish resident has been president of the Stamford Chamber of Commerce for a number of years. They take a prominent part in every civic endeavor, participating wholeheartedly in the various community drives as those for the Community Chest and Red Cross, and contributing generously to their funds.

Probably no other group, however, shows as much concern with and responsibility for its fellow members as the Jewish. None is refused aid when in need, and, as will be shown presently, few resort to general local charity. The Jewish community carries the main burden of the support of the unfortunate in its midst and does it as a matter of duty as well as of pride. We have seen that when the settlement consisted of but a handful of families, agencies were set up to care for the destitute. The *Gemilat Hesed* (Free Loan Society) and *Hachnasat Orehim* (Society for Sheltering Transients) were and are taking care of the poor in all kinds of ways. The mutual benefit societies as well as other organizations and institutions, particularly the Hebrew Ladies Educational League and the synagogues, often come to the support of individuals who are not members. They all respond to any of the drives that are undertaken in behalf of the poor. Funds are collected not only for the local poor but for needy Jews everywhere.

The manner in which the two old institutions, the *Gemilat Hesed* and *Hachnasat Orehim,* operate has already been described. Aside from these, there exists a women's organization, the Hebrew Ladies Educational League, mentioned at another juncture, whose primary concern is local charity. Its name is misleading because it was originally organized mainly as an auxiliary to the Hebrew school, aiming to supplement its educational fund. Although it is still one of the chief financial supporters of the Hebrew school, it is also the most active charitable organization in the Jewish community. The League, consisting almost totally of foreign-born women, gets its funds mainly from membership dues and various affairs it runs. Prior to the High Holy Days it resorts to the ancient custom of preparing holy wax candles which are sold to individuals and lighted in the synagogue on the eve of *Yom Kippur* in memory of the departed relatives. The manner in which these candles are manufactured is interesting, particularly since it is still a prevailing practice. With the approach of the High Holy Days, a few of the most religious members of the organization visit the Jewish cemetery and measure the graves of deceased pious men and women with a cotton thread while uttering appropriate prayers. This thread is then taken to the home of one of the women and used as wicks in the making of the candles. The sales of such candles usually nets the organization over $500 a year.

PARADE ON ATLANTIC STREET, THE MAIN BUSINESS STREET OF STAMFORD IN THE 1930'S
Among the many Jewish owned businesses were — Mantell & Martin, H. Frankel & Son, and B.T. Harris Real Estate.

The charitable work carried on by the League among the needy Jewish families in town follows the traditional way of giving assistance secretly. A committee of three is in charge of the actual distribution of aid. These women have their own ways of discovering those in distress. They then visit these families, bringing them help in the form most suitable to their individual needs at the time. Assistance is given in cash, food supplies, and clothing. Sometimes aid is rendered in the form of rent payment, the repair of a truck, providing a chicken or other delicacy for a special diet, etc. All transactions of this kind are kept in the greatest of secrecy, not even members of the organization having access to the records. The work of the League is supplemented by another smaller group which is active prior to the Passover holidays. Again, following tradition, two or three individuals of the group visit Jewish homes and business places collecting money for buying matsot (the ritual unleavened bread) and other special provisions for the poor. This fund is referred to by its traditional name of *maot-hittin* (money for wheat).

Few of the needy Jewish families resort directly to general local charity. As disclosed by Table 12, of a total of 2,956 cases taken care of by the Stamford Family Welfare during a period of six years, 1932-37, only 42 or 1.42 per cent were Jewish. The Town Welfare Department has kept no record of the various ethnic groups represented on its relief rolls up to July, 1938. On that date the total number of cases on direct and supplementary relief, as disclosed by the department, was 1,789. Of these 22 belonged to the Jewish group.

Aside from local charity, the Jewish community has been contributing generously to the various funds and collections for

TABLE 12
NON-JEWISH AND JEWISH RELIEF CASES CARED FOR
BY THE STAMFORD FAMILY WELFARE, 1932-1937

Year	Total Cases	Jewish	Per Cent of Total
All Years	2,956	42	1.42
1932	532	3	0.56
1933	604	9	1.49
1934	620	11	1.77
1935	577	8	1.39
1936	341	5	1.47
1937	282	6	2.13

needy coreligionists everywhere. In the early period it was for the Russian pogrom victims that the members of the community gave readily their pennies and dollars. During the War they donated, for a period of two years, $350 every month toward the relief of distressed Jews in Europe and Palestine. In the post-War period they responded generously to the call for funds from different national agencies. And at the present, as we have seen in the preceding chapter, they contribute thousands of dollars annually to the United Jewish Appeal drives, a goodly part of which goes for the relief of poverty-stricken Jews in Europe. Many individuals in the community also obligate themselves to support various Jewish state and national institutions, such as the Home for the Aged and the Children's Home in New Haven and the Tuberculosis Sanatorium in Denver, Colorado. Frequently during the year the community is visited by emissaries from various educational, religious, and charitable institutions in Europe and Palestine, and none is sent away empty-handed. Many a Jewish home has a tin box, distributed by such an institution, hanging in its kitchen or dining room in which members of the family drop a coin whenever charitably inclined. These boxes are emptied by an agent of the particular institution on his annual or semi-annual visit to the community.

The Jews of Stamford contributed a most negligible share to crime. The data given below are based on a thorough search of the records kept in the Stamford Detective Bureau. Of the 651 persons, all residents of Stamford, convicted for both major and minor offenses in the ten-year period of 1928-1937, only 13, or 2 per cent, were Jews. As the Jews form about 5 per cent of the town's population, their criminality is much below expectation. Only in five of the ten years covered were there any cases of Jewish convictions; in 1928 there was 1, in 1930 there were 5, in 1932 — 2, in 1933 — 1, and in 1937 — 4. Although 47 of those convicted were females, none belonged to the Jewish group. Furthermore, none of the cases, as is apparent from Table 13, was of a serious nature. The year 1930 shows the largest number of Jewish offenders, namely five, but as noted in the same Table, all were convicted for "breach of peace" or "assault" during a May Day observance. Nine of the thirteen individuals were of foreign birth, but this is of no significance, since five of those nine, as pointed out, got into difficulties because of the aforementioned demonstration.

TABLE 13
CRIMINAL CASES OF JEWISH RESIDENTS IN STAMFORD
BY SEX, AGE, NATIVITY, AND TYPE OF OFFENSE, 1928-37

Year	Male	Female	Age	Country of Birth	Crime
1928	1	—	27	United States	Keeping House of Ill Fame
1929	—	—	—	—	—
1930	1	—	35	Russia	Assault*
	1	—	39	Russia	Breach of Peace*
	1	—	19	Poland	Breach of Peace*
	1	—	44	Russia	Breach of Peace*
	1	—	23	Poland	Breach of Peace*
1931	—	—	—	—	—
1932	1	—	30	Russia	Theft
	1	—	18	United States	Attempted Burglary
1933	1	—	40	Russia	False Pretense
1934	—	—	—	—	—
1935	—	—	—	—	—
1936	—	—	—	—	—
1937	1	—	32	Russia	Breach of Peace
	1	—	27	United States	Gambling
	1	—	43	Russia	Selling Indecent Literature**
	1	—	22	United States	Selling Indecent Literature**

* Convicted for participation in May Day activities
** Convicted for selling forbidden magazines at a news stand

Juvenile delinquency also occurs very rarely in the Jewish community. Comparative figures on non-Jewish and Jewish delinquency could be obtained for only three years, covering the period between July 1, 1935, and June 30, 1938, as prior to 1935 juvenile cases were dealt with by the City Court instead of a Juvenile Court, and the records were unavailable. Table 14, based on the report of the probation officer of the Juvenile Court, shows that during the two-year period between July 1, 1935, and June 30, 1937, no cases of Jewish delinquents were recorded. In 1937-38 only 3 of a total of 290 delinquent children were Jewish. The three Jewish cases were of boys about fifteen years of age. In two instances the offenses were not serious enough, and the boys were not brought to court. The cases were disposed of by the probation officer with the cooperation of a representative of the Jewish community. The remaining case was of a more serious nature, as it involved the stealing of an automobile and prior to that petty larceny. The boy was arraigned in court, and, owing to the intervention of the Jewish Center, was sent to a Jewish reform school maintained by the Board of Jewish Guardians.

TABLE 14
NON-JEWISH AND JEWISH JUVENILE DELIQUENCY
CASES IN STAMFORD JULY 1, 1935 TO JUNE 30, 1938

Period	Total Cases	Jewish Cases	Per Cent of Total
All Years	903	3	0.33
July 1, 1935 to June 30, 1936	278	0	0.00
July 1, 1936 to June 30, 1937	335	0	0.00
July 1, 1937 to June 30, 1938	290	3	1.03

Politically the Jews of Stamford are divided between the Democratic and Republican parties. The consensus is that in the pre-depression years Jews voted largely Republican. At present Jewish Republican politicians still claim that the majority of the Jews are Republicans, while Democratic politicians maintain that they are about evenly divided between the two parties. Strictly speaking, however, there has never been a "Jewish vote" in Stamford. There have been no specifically Jewish issues involved in Stamford politics, and Jews have all along voted individually rather than as a group. At the beginning of the century there functioned in the Jewish community a political organization, the so-called Hebrew Social and Political Club, which, former members agree, was non-partisan in set-up and aim. Its primary objective, they assert emphatically, was to encourage Jewish immigrants to become American citizens. The club existed only a few years, and after its dissolution no attempt was ever made to organize a similar club.

Jews, however, have been taking a not unimportant part in the political life of the town as well as in the various phases of its administration. As early as 1910 a Jew was elected Representative to the State Legislature and two others served as Justices of the Peace, and in the year following there were added to those a member of the Board of Relief and a Grand Juror.{28} In 1913 a Stamford Jew was elected Secretary of State. During the World War, in addition to several justices of the peace, the Jewish community provided a member of the Board of Apportionment and Appropriations and the food administrator. In the post-war years one Jewish resident became Assistant Prosecuting Attorney in the City Court, another a member of the Board of Finance, a third Town Personal Tax Collector, and a fourth a Prosecuting Attorney. In more recent years members of the Jewish community have served respectively as Judge of the City Court, Sealer of Weights and Measures, City Treasurer, Special Assistant to the

Attorney General, and as members of the Board of Education. In 1936 Jews held the offices of Assistant Prosecuting Attorney, Town Treasurer, members of the Board of Education, and Special Assistant to the Attorney General. In 1937-38 members of the Jewish community served respectively as Chairman and Assistant secretary of the Board of Education, as Town Treasurer, member of the Board of Finance, Corporation Council, Assistant Prosecutor, and Representative to the State Legislature.

Thus while the Jews undoubtedly constitute a unit in the city's population, they also form an integral part of the society within which they live. They participate actively in every phase of the town's life. They think, act, and behave as their neighbors. Like any other immigrant group, they share in the cultural heritage of their ancestors, but this heritage is constantly acquiring new meanings and undergoing modifications and changes that bring it into harmony with the American environment. Their social life is still largely confined to intra-group relationships, but, as we have seen, it differs little from what is commonly called the American pattern.

EPILOGUE

THE STAMFORD JEWISH COMMUNITY TODAY

By 1991, fifty-three years after Koenig had collected his data, the Jewish population of Stamford had more than tripled: the 3,279 individuals of 1938 had grown to over 10,000. Whereas in 1938 the Jews represented only five percent of the total population of 56,765, they were now close to ten percent of the total population of 108,056.

Although no survey has been undertaken since Koenig's far-reaching sociological study, it is obvious that the Jewish population of Stamford today differs in many respects from that of 1938. These differences are manifest in several ways: the nativity and occupations of the inhabitants, their religious and social lives, the organizations to which they belong, and their relationships with the community at large.

Koenig reported in 1938 that one-third of Stamford Jews were foreign born, the majority from Russia. Today fewer than five percent are foreign born, but again Russia remains in the picture — as the native land of a growing influx of recent immigrants.

Although more than half the Jews of Stamford were active in trade and commerce in 1938, a survey taken today along the lines of Koenig's report would undoubtedly show a much smaller percentage so employed. Fewer Jews in proportion to the population own retail stores. While over one-third of the Jewish population worked "for themselves" in Koenig's day, the Jews of today are employed in a much broader spectrum of occupations and on all levels of business and corporate life. They no longer play minor or "negligible" roles in finance, real estate, and insurance. In accordance with general economic trends for the community at large, far fewer workers are employed in industry. On the other hand, Jews are still well-represented in the professions, especially in law, medicine, dentistry, accountancy, and education.

Turning to religious institutions, instead of the two congregations existing in 1938 — the orthodox Congregation Agudath Sholom and the conservative Temple Beth El — there are now eight. Koenig found 25.6% of Stamford Jewish families were affiliated with religious institutions in 1938; today more than 60% belong. The largest new congregation is the reform Temple Sinai, established in 1954.

Congregation Agudath Sholom, founded in 1889, now has a membership of over 800 families. In 1965 it moved from Grove Street to a new building on Strawberry Hill Avenue. A member of the Union of Orthodox Jewish Congregations of America, its spiritual leader is Rabbi Joseph H. Ehrenkranz; its president, Leslie Goldstein.

Temple Beth El, founded in 1920, has a membership of 650 families. It moved from Prospect Street to its new quarters on Roxbury Road in 1973. A member of the United Synagogue of America, Alex Goldman is rabbi; Ronald Gross, president.

Temple Sinai, with 360 member families, is a member of the Union of American Hebrew Congregations. It began its existence at the Grove Street Church and later moved to its new building on Lakeside Drive. Rabbi Stephen Pearce is its spiritual leader and David Cohen, its president.

The Chabad-Lubavitch, under the direction of Rabbi Yisrael Deren, is a religious and educational outreach organization dedicated to spreading the Torah in the Fairfield County area. Other religious groups in Stamford include: Chavurat Aytz Chayim (Community Jewish Life), Rabbi Mark Golub; Fellowship of Jewish Learning, Rabbi Emily Korzenik; Yeshiva Bais Binymin, Rabbi Simche Schustal; and Young Israel of Stamford, Rabbi Asher Bush.

The sisterhoods of all three of the leading congregations are extremely active organizations. The largest group is the Sisterhood of the Congregation Agudath Sholom, with 620 members. Founded in 1946, the Sisterhood has long been a catalyst for the growth of the synagogue and has made major contributions to its physical plant. The current president is Sandy Ehrenkranz.

Second in size is the Temple Beth El Sisterhood, with 290 members. Founded in 1922, its aim is to support its temple and to increase the congregant's awareness of Judaism. It is governed by a presidium consisting of Jerri Buehler, Judye Goldblatt, Phyllis Heller, Lois Hofshi, and Eileen H. Rosner.

The Sisterhood of Temple Sinai consists of 175 women. Founded in 1955, it serves as a social, educational, and community extension of the temple and also provides it with financial support. Its president is Marleen Hacker.

The three principal congregations also maintain other satellite organizations. The Men's Club of Temple Beth El is presided over by Alan Silberman and the Brotherhood of Temple Sinai by Henry Bubel. There is also a social outlet for mature singles called Singles 40+ which meets regularly at Congregation Agudath Sholom. Founded in 1986, it has a mailing list of 400. Its president is Helen Barsky.

Founded in 1916, the Jewish Community Center for many years occupied its own building on Prospect Street. Koenig noted in 1938 that, "virtually every gathering of social or cultural nature takes place within its walls." Today much of the social life of the Stamford Jewish community revolves around the Jewish Community Center of Stamford now in a magnificent new building erected on Newfield Avenue in 1981. With over 5,000 members, it is one of the largest social service agencies in Stamford and is recognized as a major contributor to the well being of the entire Stamford community.

Of the many Jewish organizations in Stamford, a number have educational objectives. Primary in this regard is the Bi-Cultural Day School. Founded in 1956 by Walter Shuchatowitz with the purpose of raising a generation of knowledgeable and committed Jews, it offers the best in secular and Judaic education. Originally at the old Jewish Community Center on Prospect Street, it moved in 1961 to the Hebrew School of Congregation Agudath Sholom and in 1982 to its own building on High Ridge Road. It has grown from ten students at its inception to 350 today and is recognized by the United states Department of Education as an exemplary school.

The Fairfield County Chapter of the Brandeis University National Women's Committee, with 400 members, is one of the largest and most active educational organizations in Stamford. Founded in 1955, its purpose is to underwrite the salaries, books, and other materials at the Brandeis University libraries. It also provides study groups and other educational opportunities for its members. Presiding over its many activities is a presidium consisting of Fran Gilmore, Bobby Jacobs, and Adele Weitzner.

The Stamford/Rippowam Chapter of Women's American ORT, founded in 1973, is affiliated with the Women's Organization for Rehabilitation through Training. With a membership of 150, its purpose is to raise money for ORT schools throughout the world. Merkaz Torah D'Stamford, also founded in 1973, provides educational and social programs for post-Bar and Bat Mitzvah teenagers. With a membership of 100, it meets on a rotating basis at Temple Beth El, Temple Sinai, and Congregation Agudath Sholom.

The Kadimah Chapter of AMIT Women was founded in 1969 to support and foster religious education for disadvantaged and troubled youth in Israel. With approximately 100 members, it has been especially active in helping Russian emigrants in Israel. AMIT is governed by a presidium consisting of Elizabeth Rosenbaum, Barbara Ashkenas, and Beth Saar.

The Fairfield County Chapter of American Friends of the Hebrew University was founded in 1985 to secure financial support for Hebrew University of Jerusalem. With a membership of seventy-five, its co-chairmen are Jeffrey K. Gallin and Morris Sandler. Elaine Sklar Davis is the Regional representative for Fairfield County.

Of the eight service organizations mentioned in Koenig's report, only two survive today: the Stamford Chapter of Haddassh, The Women's Zionist Organization of America; and Stamford Post #142 of the Jewish War Veterans of the United States. Hadassah, organized in Stamford in 1917 (although Koenig puts the date as 1924), has grown from 400 women in Koenig's time to 700 today. Founded as a voluntary organization to advance the quality of life through health and education programs, Hadassah maintains two hospitals in Israel. It also sponsors a Career Counseling Institute and the Hadassah College of Technology. There are currently four groups of Hadassah in Stamford: the Chapter, Chai, Glays Zales, and Rishona. Their respective presidents are Adele Avruch, Rhea Comen, Madeline Field, and Florence Friedman.

The Fred Robbins Post #142 of the Jewish War Veterans of the United States was founded in 1937 with Louis Altman as the first commander. Its purpose then — as it is today — was to demonstrate that Jews have served our country with honor in all wars, including the Revolution. It also combats prejudice, when it exists, at the local level. For example, when the German-American Bund created a camp in Monroe, Connecticut in 1937, members of the Post, along with a group from the American Legion, tore it apart, forcing the Bund to abandon it. Membership in the Post has grown from twenty-five to 150. Since its inception, meetings of the Post have been held at the Jewish Community Center of Stamford, first on Prospect Street and, since 1981, on Newfield Avenue. Its present commander is Nathan Davis.

In the years since 1938, many new organizations have appeared. By far the largest of these is the United Jewish Federation of Stamford, with 3000 family members. Founded in 1974, the Federation is a fund-raising and planning organization for the entire Jewish community. It also serves as an advocate on behalf of Soviet Jews and is involved in intra-faith activites. Its president is Ben Zinbarg.

Jewish Family Service, a social service organization, was founded in Stamford in 1975. Its aims are to strengthen Jewish family life, assist the elderly, and increase Jewish identity. It has resettled over 300 refugees and counseled over 500 clients. Its current president is Martin Manaly.

The Stamford Section of the National Council of Jewish Women was founded in 1951. Its membership has grown from about twenty to 350. The Council has been active in the fields of education, service, and social action. It has successfully lobbied for school bus "stop arms" as state law and has organized child care forums for corporations in the Stamford area. Its coordinators are Lonnie Sterling and Gail Trell.

B'nai B'rith, a multi-faceted community men's service organization, was founded in 1941 as Stamford Lodge #1473. It currently has eighty-two members, with co-presidents Max Friedman, Joseph Miller, and Arthur Finchler. The president of its sister orgaization, B'nai B'rith Women, is Ida Chavkin. Another B'nai B'rith group, Nutmeg unit #5325, was founded in 1962 as an alternative to Stamford lodge for younger men. Currently with 100 members, its president is Stanley Tannenbaum. B'nai B'rith has always had an interest in youth, as evidenced by two chapters of B'nai B'rith Girls in Stamford: Tikvah, with seventy menbers; and Wendy Gorman, with fifteen. Both concentrate on community service and Jewish education of the young throughout the world. The president of Tikvah is Lauren Kalter; of Gorman, Sally Lazar.

Also affiliated with B'nai B'rith is the Holocaust Memorial Committee, founded in 1975. Its objective is to commemorate the Holocaust through meetings, scholorships, and essay contests. The committee has also erected a memorial and established a Holocaust Library at the Jewish Community Center.

Another local organization is the Stamford Chapter of the National Jewish Hospital in Denver, with 100 members. Founded in 1987, its purpose is to raise funds for the Hospital. Its president is Rosalyn Weinstein.

The Adult Council for Jewish Youth, also established in 1987, coordinates programs for parents, pre-teens, and teenagers. Its concerns are youth and parental relationships. Consisting of sixteen local Jewish organizations, its co-chairs are Susan Harinstein and Hadassah Schulman.

There are also several organizations that serve wider constituencies. The Connecticut Chapter of Parents of North American Israelis (PNAI), founded in 1975, provides a link between North American parents and their children who have made Aliyah. There are about 100 family members, including twenty from Stamford.

The Jewish Home for the Elderly of Fairfield County, founded in Bridgeport in the late 1960s, moved to Fairfield in 1973. With a membership of 4,500, it has a national reputation for excellence. The Home, with 360 beds, provides skilled nursing care for the frail Jewish elderly. It also provides two day care programs for older adults, two dementia units, a child care center, Meals-on-Wheels, and teaches religious and health care professionals of the future.

The Stamford Jewish Historical Society was founded in 1983 by nine individuals with Irwin Miller as president. It promotes research, preservation, collection, and education relating to the Jewish community's history. Ten meetings are held each year with speakers on local, United States, and world Jewish history, culture, and arts. In addition, it maintains archives of records and artifacts. The Society was responsible for the creation of the "Dr. Jacob Nemoitin, Healer and Humanitarian," Exhibit which was on display at the Stamford Historical Society, The Jewish Community Center and the Mayor's Gallery at the Government Center. The society's major current project is publishing the late Samuel Koenig's report. There are now 270 members with Greoge Goldberg as president.

In addition to the rich diversity of interest in Judaism documented above, the Stamford Jewish community has remained a dynamic force in the city. Koenig said of the Jews of Stamford: "They form an integral part of the society within which they live. They participate actively in every phase of the town's life. They think, act, and behave as their neighbors."

His eloquent words ring out today as resoundingly as they did fifty-three years ago.

APPENDIX A

ARTICLES OF INCORPORATION OF
CONGREGATION AGUDATH SHOLOM

(From Stamford Town Records, Book No. 71, Page 63)

Stamford Conn, July 1889. On this date, we the undersigned members of our congregation "Agudath-Shalom" (Knot of Peace), have finished paing for the "Thora" (Bible) and other things which belong to the service; that amount to Seventy-five (75) dollars (as the enclosed receipt of Mr. A. L. Germansky, of whom the things were bought; ratifies the fact.) And as this holly deed of ours, shall never be forgotten from us, and our forthcomings; we resolved upon the following points: 1, That the name of this Congregation shall forever be "Agudath-Shalom". 2, The valuables of this congregation is only for Stamford, Conn. defined, and shall not be never removed from here. 3, In case, if our members, shall be reduced to less than five; the remaining four or less (of now existing ones): will only then have the privilege of using the "Thora" and the rest of the things belonging to it, if they will give security for executing the aforesaid points; but if they will fail to give the aforesaid security, the "Thora" shall be sent to New York City Norfolk Str. Synaguge in a month's time. 4, Children and brothers of the undersigned members have in the aforesaid points, the same right as the members themselves, i.e. if they only wish to belong to the same congregation "Agudath-Shalom". 5, This document shall be undersigned by the Stamford Conn. town-lawyer or at the Notary Public. 6, The number of the house and the name of the man, where the "Thora" and the other things, which belong to the service will be found, must be at one informed by the aforesaid lawyer or at the Notary Public in case of removal. And, 7, to have this document undersigned by the town-lawyer or at the Notary-Public, we apoint Mr. Jacob Rosenblum.

Stamford Conn. July 1889
1. JOSEPH NACHEMSON YIDDISH SIGNATURE
2. JACOB ROSENBLUM
3. ADOLPH JAFFA
4. DAVIS COHEN
5. WOLF GREENBERG YIDDISH SIGNATURE
6. SOLAMAN OSMUNSKI
7. ARON BROCKAIN
8. LEWIS SPELKE
9. MOSES GORDAN
10. B. OSMANSKY
11. ISIDOR ZARP
12. ISRAEL F. GOLDSTEIN YIDDISH SIGNATURE
13. AVNER RABINOWITZ YIDDISH SIGNATURE
14. JOSEPH FROMMER YIDDISH SIGNATURE
15. SHEPE BEHRMAN YIDDISH SIGNATURE
16. ABRAHM MULARNIK YIDDISH SIGNATURE
17. SOLOMAN ABRAHAMS YIDDISH SIGNATURE
18. ELIE GORDON
19. A. KRIGER YIDDISH SIGNATURE
20. ALCH. GOLDBERG
21. MOSES RUBUNOCK YIDDISH SIGNATURE
22. CH. OLSHWANGER YIDDISH SIGNATURE

Received for Record September 7, 1889 at 3 o'clock P.M. and recorded by Charles E. Holly, Town Clerk.

Note: above copied from Dr. Koenig's typescript including errata.

APPENDIX B

ARTICLES OF ASSOCIATION OF
AGUDATH SHOLOM CEMETERY

(From Stamford Town Records, Book No. 75, Page 250

Be it Known, That we the subscribers, residents of the Town of Stamford, in Fairfield County Connecticut, do hereby associate ourselves as a body politic and corporate, pursuant to the Statute laws of the State of Connecticut, regulating the formation and organization of burying grounds and Cemetery Associations, for the purpose of procuring and establishing a cemetery or place of supulture, and the following are our articles of Association.

ART. 1 — The name of said corporation shall be the Agoodat Solima Cemetery Association.

ART. 2 — The Statute laws of the State of Connecticut relating to cemetery associations are hereby particularly referred to and made part of these articles, and the corporation hereby organized and established under and pursuant to said Statute laws shall have all the powers and proceed according to the regulations described and specified therein.

ART. 3 — The said corporation shall be located in the Town of Stamford in Fairfield County, Connecticut.

ART. 4 — The management of said association shall be vested in a Board of Trustees, consisting of members of the association, all of whom shall be residents of Stamford, who shall be elected in the following manner.

At the semi-annual meeting of the Association on August 23rd. the year 1891 there shall be elected by ballot Three Trustees to serve six months each and at each semi-annual meeting of the Association there-after there shall be elected by ballot Three Trustees to serve six months each.

Any vacancy occuring in the Board of Trustees between the semi-annual meetings of the Association may be filled by a majority vote of the Trustees present at any regularly called meeting of the board.

ART. 5 — The Association shall at its semi-annual meeting elect from among its members a President, a Vice-President, a Secretary and a Treasurer, who may hold office for the term of six months and until their successors shall have been elected.

ART. 6 — The semi-annual meetings of the Association shall be held in Stamford on the 23rd. of August and the 23rd. day of February in each year.

Special meetings of the Association may be called at any time by the President, and shall be called by the President or the Secretary upon the written request of any two of the Trustees or upon the written request of ten members of the Association.

Notice of all meetings of the Association, stating time and place of meeting, shall be given by publication in two or more of the newspapers published in Stamford, at least three days prior to the date of each meeting.

ART. 7 — The Board of Trustees shall have the general management of the funds and property of the Association; shall cause the grounds of said Association to be graded, and the same to be laid out into proper ways, roads and plots; shall fix the price to be paid for lots in the cemetery, and shall dispose of the same as they deem expedient.

The Treasurer shall keep the funds of said Association subject to the order of the Board of Trustees; and the Secretary shall keep a true record of all the proceedings of this Association and the necessary books.

ART. 8 — The Trustees shall have power to make and adopt such by-laws, rules and regulations as may be found necessary for the proper management of the affairs of the Association and for the proper care and preservation of its property. But any such by-laws, rules or regulations may be amended or repealed by a majority vote of the members of the Association present, in person or by proxy, at any semi-annual or special meeting of the Association, notice of such proposed alteration to be printed in the call of such meeting.

ART. 9 — The owner or proprietor of any lot or lots may transfer the same under such rules and regulations as may by adopted by the Association.

ART. 10 — These Articles of Association may be altered or amended by a two-third vote of the members of the Association present, in person or by proxy, at a meeting called for such purpose; notice of such meeting stating its object having been given by publication in two or more of the newspapers published in Stamford, for two weeks prior to the date of such meeting.

ART. 11 — All persons who are subscribers to these Articles and all persons who may be admitted by vote of the members at any regular meeting and all persons who may hereafter become lot owners under the rules, by-laws or regulations of this Association shall be members of said Association, and each of the persons so becoming members shall be entitled to one vote in any election or meeting of the Association.

ART. 12 — Any officer of the Association may be removed from office by a two-third vote of the members present at any meeting of the Association, provided that the call for such meeting shall set forth the intent and purpose to take such action.

ART. 13 — Any member failing or refusing to comply with the rules, by laws or regulations of the Association or failing to pay such assessments or dues as may be required by the by-laws or vote of the Association may be expelled from membership therein in such a manner and by such proceeding as the Association may by by-law provide.

Dated at Stamford August 21, 1891

J. NACHMANSON
S. GARTMAN
IKE HERRON
MORRIS KRONBAHK
ADOLPH JAFFA
M. BROODMAN
I. GOLDSTEIN
JACOB ROSENBLUME
D. COHEN
L.
SAM ABRAHAM
JOE WOLPAN
MORRIS GORDON
JOSEPH BLUM
J. MOLL
A. SHPAHKA
J. PHILIP

We, the undersigned, a majority of the directors of the Agoodat Solima Cemetery Association hereby certify that the foregoing is a true copy of the Articles of Association of the said corporation, and of the names of the subscribers threto.

SAML. GORTMAN
President
JOE BLUM
Vice President
M. GORDON   A majority of Trustees
Secy.
LEWIS SPELPE
Trustee
JOS. PHILLIPS
Trustee

State of Connecticut
Fairfield County   S.S. Stamford, August 26th, 1891

Then and there personally appeared Sam Gortman, Pres. Joe Blum, V. Pres. M. Gordon, Secy. J. Nachmanson & L. Spelke, J. Philip, a majority of the Trustees of the Agoodat Salima Cemetery Association, and made oath to the truth of the foregoing certificate before.

MICHAEL KENEALY
Commissioner of the Superior Court for Fairfield County

Received for record Sept. 2, 1891 at 10.20 A.M. and recorded by WILLIAM F. WATERBURY Town Clerk

APPENDIX C

AGUDATH SHOLOM CEMETERY DEED

(From Stamford Town Records, Book No. 75, Page 459)

To all People to whom these Presents shall come, greetings know ye that I, REBECCA FAIRCHILD OF STAMFORD, FAIRFIELD COUNTY, CONNECTICUT

For the consideration of ONE HUNDRED AND SEVENTY-FIVE ($175) DOLLARS received to MY full satisfaction of THE AGOODAT SOLEINA CEMETERY ASSOCIATION A CORPO-RATION LEGALLY ORGANIZED UNDER THE LAWS OF THIS STATE AND LOCATED IN SAID STAMFORD do give, grant, bargain, sell and confirm unto the said ASSOCIATION, ALL THAT CERTAIN TRACT OF LAND LYING IN SAID STAMFORD IN QUANTITY TWO ACRES MORE OR LESS AND BOUNDED NORTH AND WEST BY LAND OF THE ESTATE OF PATRICK O'NEIL DECEASED, EAST BY HIGH-WAY AND SOUTH BY MAPLE SWAMP, SO CALLED.

To have and to hold the above granted and bargained pre-mises, with the appurtenances thereof unto the said grantee ITS SUCCESSORS and assigns forever, to ITS and their own proper use and behoof. And also I the said grantor do for MY SELF MY heirs, executors, and administrators, covenant with the said GRANTEE, ITS SUCCESSORS and assigns that at and until the ensealing OF these presents I AM well seized of the premises as a good inefeasible estate in fee simple, and have good right to bargain and sell the same in manner and form as is above writ-ten; and that the same is free from all incumbrances whatsoever.

And furthermore, I the said grantor do by these presents bind BY SELF and MY heirs forever, to warrant and defend the above granted and bargained premises to IT the said grantee

ITS SUCCESSORS heirs and assigns against all claims and demands whatsoever.

In witness whereof, I have hereunto set MY hand and seal THIS 2ND day of SEPTEMBER A.D., 1891. Signed, Sealed and Delivered in presence of

M. KENEALY	her
	Rebecca X Fairchild
C.H. WOLFE	mark

State of Connecticut
County of Fairfield   SS,: STAMFORD, SEPT. 2ND A.D., 1891

Personally appeared REBECCA FAIRCHILD

Signer and Sealer of the foregoing Instrument, and acknowledged the same to be HER free Act and Deed, before me

Commissioner of the Superior Court
MICHAEL KENEALY   for FAIRFIELD County.

Received for Record SEPT. 2, 1891 AT 10:25 AM and recorded by

WILLIAM F. WATERBURY, TOWN CLERK

Note: above copied from Dr. Koenig's typescript including errata.

APPENDIX D

DEED OF SALE OF
AGUDATH SHOLOM SYNAGOGUE LOT

(From Stamford Town Records, Book No. 106, Page 259)

To all People to whom these Presents shall come, greeting

Know Ye That THE GREYROCK LAND COMPANY, A CORPORATION AND ORGANIZED AND EXISTING UNDER THE LAWS OF THE STATE OF CONNECTICUT, AND LOCATED AT STAMFORD, FAIRFIELD COUNTY, CONNECTICUT, BY FRANCIS S. HOYT, OF MORRISTOWN, MORRIS COUNTY, NEW JERSEY, ITS PRESIDENT, HEREUNTO DULY AUTHORIZED, for the consideration of ONE DOLLAR received to ITS full satisfaction of THE HEBREW CONGREGATION AGUDAS SHOLEM, AN ECCLESIASTICAL CORPORATION, LOCATED AT STAMFORD, FAIRFIELD COUNTY, CONNECTICUT, do give, grant, bargain, sell and confirm unto the said THE HEBREW CONGREGATION AGUDAS SHOLEM ALL THAT CERTAIN LOT OF LAND SITUATED IN SAID STAMFORD ON GREYROCK PLACE AND BOUNDED NORTHERLY ONE HUNDRED AND FIVE 15/100 (105.15) FEET BY LAND OF THE GRANTOR, EASTERLY TWENTY-NINE 12/100 (29.12) FEET BY SAID GREYROCK PLACE, SOUTHERLY ONE HUNDRED AND TWO 35/100 102.35) FEET BY LAND OF THE GRANTOR, LAID OUT AND USED AS AN ALLEY AND WESTERLY THIRTY-SEVEN 43/100 (37.43) FEET BY SAID LAND OF THE GRANTOR USED AS AN ALLEY AS AFORESAID LEADING FROM GREYROCK PLACE ALONGSIDE OF LAND OF THE SWEDISH M.E. CHURCH TO THE REAR OF LOTS BELONGING TO SAID GREYROCK LAND COMPANY FACING ON SAID GREYROCK PLACE.

SAID PREMISES TO BE USED FOR THE PURPOSE OF A SYNAGOGUE.

To Have And To Hold the above granted and bargained premises, with the appurtances thereof unto IT the said grantee ITS SUCCESSORS heirs and assigns forever to their own proper use and behoof. And also the said grantor does for ITSELF, ITS SUCCESSORS, executors, and administrators, covenant with the said grantee ITS SUCCESSORS and assigns that at, and until the ensealing of these presents IT IS well seized of the premises as a good indefeasible estate in fee simple, and have good right to bargain and sell the same in manner and form as is above written; and that the same is free from all incumbrances whatsoever.

And Furthermore, the said grantor does by these presents bind ITSELF and ITS SUCCESSORS forever, to warrant and defend the above granted and bargained premises to the said grantee ITS SUCCESSORS and assigns against all claims and demands whatsoever.

In Witness Whereof THE SAID THE GREYROCK LAND COMPANY, BY ITS PRESIDENT, AFORESAID, HAS HERE-UNTO SET IS CORPORATE NAME AND AFFIXED ITS SEAL THIS 7TH DAY OF OCTOBER A.D. 1903

Signed, Sealed and Delivered
   in presence of

KATHL. R. HART   THE GREYROCK LAND CO.

                              (L.S.)

MARTIN J. GRAY   BY FRANCIS S. HOYT, PREST.

State of Connecticut   S.S.STAMFORD, OCT. 7TH, A.D., 1903

Personally appeared THE GREYROCK LAND COMPANY BY FRANCIS S. HOYT, ITS PRESIDENT Signer and Sealer of the foregoing Instrument WHO acknowledged the same to be HIS free Act and Deed, AND THE FREE ACT AND DEED OF SAID THE GREYROCK LAND COMPANY, BEFORE ME.

KATHL. R. HART, NOTARY PUBLIC FOR CONN.

Received for Record AUG. 10, 1904, 12.00M and recorded by

WILLIAM T. WATERBURY Town Clerk

ADDENDA

ADDITIONAL HISTORICAL NOTES
ADDED BY IRWIN MILLER

In the text these notes are enclosed in { } symbols.

1. Jacob Hart settled in Stamford in 1732, raised a family and remained in Stamford until 1764. Some others were Samuel and Miriam Levy in 1747-8, and during the Revolutionary War between 1776 and 1785 the families of Manuel Myers and Isaac Pinto. Also, from 1804-6 there were the Gomez and Lopez families. Page 16

2. The majority of early Jewish settlers in Connecticut were of Ashkenazic rather than Sephardic origin. These were individuals with names of Hays, Hart, Isaacs, Levy, Marks, Myers, Simpson, and Trubee. Page 16

3. Early Jews in Stamford were Jacob Fox, 1859; Wolff Cohen, 1862; Maurice Benas and Ralph Benjamin, 1865; Tobias and Henry Bernhard, 1868; Isaac Fox, 1869; Samuel Cohen, 1870; Elchana Carensky, 1870; Leopold Frank, 1872; Charles Fox, 1875; Peter Fox, 1876, and in 1879 Jacob Desky, Charles Weinstein, and Simon and Samuel Shulz and their immediate families. Wolff Cohen was born in Warsaw, a part of Poland then controlled by Czarist Russia. Tobias and Henry Bernhard were also born in Poland, Lucynow. Page 16

4. Isaac and Bertha Fox with daughter Rachel are listed in the 1870 U.S. Census of Stamford. An advertisement in 1904 states he established a liquor business thirty-five years before, 1869. Isaac and Jacob Fox were brothers. Charles and Peter Fox were also brothers, but their relationship to Isaac and Jacob is not known. The 1880 U.S. Census of Stamford indicates Charles and Peter Fox with their families arrived in 1875 and 1876, respectively. All were married when they arrived in Stamford. Page 18

5. The 1870 U.S. Census of Stamford indicates Wolff and Harriet Cohen arrived in 1862 with their children Rachel, Samuel, Byron, Leonard, and Albert. Page 18

6. Samuel H. Cohen, an attorney, was the son of Wolff and married Kitty around 1877. Page 18

7. This Samuel Cohen, a dry goods merchant, was listed as Kohen in the 1870 census. Page 18

8. See note 3, above. Page 18

9. Wolff Cohen was from Warsaw, Poland and Tobias and Henry Bernhard were from Lucynow, Poland. Page 18

10. The Rabbi was Henry Vidaver of orthodox congregation B'nai Jeshurum of New York City. Page 18

11. The Cohen families all left Stamford by 1885 for New York City, prior to the founding of any Jewish institutions. The mother tongue of the new arrivals in the 1880s was Yiddish, unlike that of the earlier arrivals, such as the Foxes, making communication and culture different. Tobias Bernhard who arrived in 1868 was a member of Jacob Ullman Lodge B'nai Brith which was founded in 1910. Joseph Moll, a native of Cincinnati, Ohio, arrived in Stamford in 1885 and is listed as a director of Agudath Sholom Cemetery at its founding in 1891. Page 19

12. Samuel Cohen who owned a dry goods store on Atlantic Street in 1870 was married to Mary and had two children. He left Stamford for New York City in 1880. Samuel H. Cohen, the lawyer, was married to Kitty and she had a millinery shop in her father-in-law's Wolff Cohen's clothing store at 7 Park Row. Page 19

13. This refers to Jacob Fox Senior and not Isaac Fox. The son mentioned is Jacob Fox Junior. Page 20

14. Henry apparently did not survive as he is not mentioned in the 1870 census. Page 20

15. The last Fox, Regina Fox, left Stamford in 1912. Page 20

16. Henry and Rachel Bernhard settled in Middletown, Connecticut in 1872. Their great-grandson, Harry Bernhard, was president of Stamford's Temple Sinai in 1979. Page 20

17. Jacob Rosenbloom in 1881. Page 20

18. Norwalk did not have a congregation during the Revoltionary War. Hazan Seixas settled in Stratford in 1776 and remained there until 1780 when he was called to Philadelphia. Seixas did conduct services in Stratford where his parents were living during that period. There were enough Jews for a minyan. Page 20

19. Jews of German speaking origin in the Stamford of 1879 were counted as German; this included those of Prussian-Polish birth. Page 22

20. Abraham Cohen was a native of Prussia, unlike most of the other settlers of that period, was listed in 1891 as a cigar maker living on Court Street. The Stamford City Directory of 1883 lists Marks Myeh as a peddler, Harry and Sarah Moseman, salesman, Max Meyrech, peddler, Gustave Mayer, tailor, Edward Stern, owner of woolen mill on W. Main Street, Charles Weinstein, carriage painter, Henry Adleman, painter, Isadore Alexander, peddler, Louis H. Levinson, dry goods on Park Row. Some of these named were also Eastern-European Jews and this is by no means a complete listing. Page 25

21. No mention is made of other settlers such as Sigismund Kronholtz, jeweler and clockmaker of 1888. Some of them stayed a few years and moved on; see Stamford City Directories. In 1885, Saul Adams opened his first clothing store in the Stamford House Hotel. In 1892, he sold out to the Martin brothers and became a realtor and builder. According to David Cohen's memoirs, he was extremely helpful to the new immigrants in organizing the first High Holy Day Services and in resolving any difficulties they may have had with the civil authorities. Page 26

22. David Cohen in his memoirs mentions the arrival of a shochet named Smith with his family from Canada in 1887. Smith was shochet, chicken slaughterer, and would go to New York City twice a week to obtain herring and kosher meats for sale to the community. He also supplied the shofar for the first High Holy Day Services in 1887. Page 32

23. Now known as Independent Stamford Lodge. Page 37

24. The 1905 City Directory and through 1917, Morris Francovitch is listed first as "Pastor" and later as Rabbi of Congregation Agudath Sholom. He also owned a dry goods store on Pacific Street. In 1918, Rabbi Nathan Shapiro is listed as the congregation's spiritual leader. Page 41

25. The founder and president of Norma-Hoffman was Walter Marks Nones, a Jew. Harold J. Ritter, also Jewish succeeded him as president of the company. Page 71

26. Now known as Fred Robbins Post #142. Page 117

27. Benjamin T. Harris arrived in Stamford in 1899. Page 139

28. Albert Phillips (1887-1925), an attorney and protegé of Homer S. Cummings. He was a member of the law firm of Cummings and Lockwood from 1908 to 1910. Page 145

ADDENDA

INDEX

From the New York Times, December 31, 1972

Samuel Koenig, Sociologist, Dies
Author, 73, was Department Head at Brooklyn College

Dr. Samuel Koenig, chairman of the department of sociology and anthropology at Brooklyn college from 1948 to 1965, died Friday in Lenox Hill Hospital. He was 73 years old and lived at 1890 East 21st Street Brooklyn.

Dr. Koenig was the author of the textbook Sociology: an Introduction to the Science of Society, which has been translated into Hebrew, Chinese, and Bengali.

He was born in Galicia, Austria, and came to the United States in 1921. He studied at the University of Minnesota, graduated from Marquette University in 1929 and received a Ph.D degree from Yale in 1935.

After directing sociology studies for the Connecticut Federal Writers Project from 1936 to 1941, he joined Brooklyn College, from which he retired as professor in 1970.

Dr. Koenig had been a Fulbright professor at Bar-Illan University in Israel in 1957-58; Karnatak University in India, 1964-65, and Osmania University, also in India, 1968-69.

He served on the National Commission on Hebrew Language and Culture, on the Commission for the Study of Jewish Education in the United States and on the council of the Yivo Institute for Jewish Research. In 1950 he studied cultural trends in Israel under a grant from the Social Science research Council.

Among his books are *Jews in a Gentile World, The Refugees Are Now Americans, One America, Contemporary Sociology,* and *The Sociology of Crime.*